C

ESSAYS IN
SOCIOECONOMIC EVOLUTION

ESSAYS IN SOCIOECONOMIC EVOLUTION

Morris A. Copeland
Professor of Economics Emeritus
Cornell University

VANTAGE PRESS
New York / Washington / Atlanta
Los Angeles / Chicago

FIRST EDITION

Published by Vantage Press, Inc.
516 West 34th Street, New York, New York 10001

Manufactured in the United States of America
Standard Book Number 533-04328-X

Library of Congress Catalog Card No.: 79-65045

Contents

Preface

Each of the six papers in this little volume is concerned with a segment of economic history or, in the case of the paper on the two nonpecuniary civilizations, with two segments. They are all written from a common viewpoint. In each of them, the writer has been thinking of the developments with which it is dealing as a portion of a natural evolutionary process, a step or stage in the evolution of social and economic institutions.

Probably every economist and every econometrician today has been enough influenced by Charles Darwin's *Origin of Species* to think that men and other mammals are products of organic evolution, that they are descended from a common ancestor. But some economists and some econometricians do not accept the logical corollary of this proposition, viz., that our economy is a product of socioeconomic evolution. Some of them believe that there are principles of economics or laws of economics that have a validity like the validity of Euclidean geometry. A single example may suffice. Frank H. Knight thought of economics as "a science of principles," "principles that are not different in different culture situations—exactly as the principles of mathematics are not different."*

Economists are agreed that economics is a science. But there is wide disagreement on what it means to call economics

---

*These words are quoted from a critical comment he made on Melville J. Herskovits's *Economic Anthropology*. Herskovits reports the comment in his appendix. Of course, Herskovits in this book is concerned with socioeconomic evolution.

a science, and on its place among the sciences. It may be well, therefore, to say what this writer means by saying that it is a natural science. He means that he considers it a branch of biology. As such, it is concerned with the behavior of man as a gregarious mammal. It is concerned with cause-and-effect sequences and stimulus-response patterns in his behavior. Like physiology, it makes use of a concept of a teleological character; it is concerned to identify the functions of various things that man's activities involve; for example, the functions of money. And it is concerned with a feature of animal behavior that is essentially peculiar to man; it is concerned with his institutions.

The word institution in this sense is not easy to define. An insitituion is a complicated set of related behavior patterns that characterize the members of a culture group or of a group of persons with a common historical background. The institution that most completely dominates the activities of any culture group is its language. Among the economic institutions dealt with in these six papers are: property, contract, the price system, and the wage system.

Much speculation is doubtless unscientific. But speculation is also appropriate in a scientific inquiry. In these six papers, the writer has engaged extensively in speculations; but he has sought to confine them to the making of hypotheses that lend themselves to empirical exploration. Such hypotheses are not only appropriate in a scientific inquiry; but they are also the principal means of adding to our scientific knowledge.

One type of judgment that has no proper place in a scientific inquiry into developments in human institutions is a judgment that asserts a moral approval or disapproval of a development. Many historians seem to think it their business to make such judgments, for example, to concern themselves with progress. The writer has been studiously careful to avoid making any such judgment.

One of the six economic history papers, "Concerning the Origin of a Money Economy," delves into prehistory. Four of them and one part of a fifth are exclusively concerned with ancient history. Only two of them have to do with developments since 1400 A.D.

The lives of two individuals, Alexander the Great and Hippocrates, are touched on in two of the papers. But for the most part attention is focused not on personalities but on impersonal developments, new knowledge, technological innovations, changes in institutions.

The writer has been especially interested in what is called cultural borrowing, the adoption of the culture traits of one civilization by another civilization. The paper on "Developments in Military Technology and Government Organization in the Ancient Near East" gives a good deal of attention to this kind of borrowing and the interpretation of history Thorstein Veblen proposes for dealing with it.

There are a number of proper nouns the English versions of which take different forms in different books. In general, the form adopted here is that adopted in the 1968 *Encyclopaedia Britannica*. Where the alternative forms are markedly different, the first time a noun occurs the form adopted here is followed by the alternative or alternatives in parentheses, thus: Erech (Uruk, Warka). There are two nouns for which different articles in the 1968 *Encyclopaedia* follow different usages. In the paper on the "The Economics of the Two Great Nonpecuniary Civilizations," the Indians who had a great empire in western South America are referred to as Incas and the official language of the empire as *Quechua*.

The Oxford University Press has kindly given permission to include in this book a photographic copy of a picture that appears in C. Leonard Woolley's book, *The Sumerians,* a picture of one side of the mosaic known as the Standard of Ur. The mosaic is now in the British Museum. The photographic copy shown here is made from page 51 of the reprinting of Woolley's book by W. W. Norton & Company, Inc., in 1965. The permission given by Oxford University Press is gratefully acknowledged. The assistance of W. W. Norton & Company, Inc., in making this arrangement is also gratefully acknowledged.

The permission given by the American Journal of Economics and Sociology to reprint in *Essays in Socioeconomic Evolution* two papers the Journal has published is gratefully acknowledged. One of them, "Concerning the Origin of a Money Economy," appeared in the January 1974 issue; the other, "Foreign Exchange in the Eastern Mediterranean in the Fourth Century B.C.," appeared in the April 1977 issue.

Morris A. Copeland
Venice, Florida
April, 1979

Foreword

The economy of our advanced industrial society that feeds, clothes and shelters us and provides all the amenities that help to make life worth living, is a part of that complex of institutions that comprise our culture, the secret of human survival. If we are to understand that economy, we must know all we can learn about the origins of its institutions as well as about their development and functioning. For it is in the nature of institutions—indeed, it is their reason for being—to hand down the past to the future. The present, of course, is never identical with the past. But it never succeeds in severing its ties to the past. Nothing is more practical than the study of our origins together with the study of our development. It is the way we can understand how we came to be what we are.

This sounds like a plea for the study of history and I would not mind if it were taken as such. For history, in this case, economic history, is essential to a science of economics. But many of our economic institutions antedate recorded history, and so their origins cannot be studied by the historical method. For information about them, it is necessary to turn to what the student of the social sciences must consider exotic sciences, for example, archaeology and paleography and linguistics. But here we run afoul of our vaunted specialization, which, while it is responsible for the great advances in science of the last hundred years, also tends to put blinders on our seeing. The archaeologist painstakingly gathers the relevant artifacts but lacks the economic training needed to interpret their significance meaningfully. This requires the expertise of the economist.

This is precisely what Morris Copeland brings to the study of economic institutions in ancient times reported in this book, his *Essays in Socioeconomic Evolution:* the expertise of the economist (together with that firm foundation for technical training, the basic education in the liberal arts that used to be the hallmark of the cultivated person). Of course, he has no intention of displacing the archaeologist or his brethren; the past, as it may be known by its relics or other survivals, is theirs without dispute. But the economist of proper background can help the archaeologist to interpret his finds. For many years, from my watchtower as a science journalist, I have been a keen observer of the scientific enterprise. In my view, it is the kind of cooperation in which Morris Copeland has been willing to engage that has been responsible for many of our recent advances.

And it is altogether fitting that it should be Morris Copeland who is the economist who undertakes that kind of cooperation. For he is a member of the institutionalist school of economic thought, and the founder of that point of view, Thorstein Veblen, believed that the proper study of economic institutions began with their origins in the early Stone Age. I never knew Veblen; when I began my studies at the New School for Social Research, he had already left the faculty. But he was still a living memory there, as he continued to be even when the influx of refugee scholars from Europe gave his influence competition. And the late Helen Slade, who (with Gerhard Colm) was my sponsor among the statisticians, had not only been a pupil of Veblen's but was one of his staunchest admirers. Veblen was, indeed, interested in the evolution of institutions, so much so that today an alternative name for the school is evolutionary economics. But he also had a keen interest in their origins, an interest shared by few of his present-day followers. This, I think, is regrettable for—to cite only one reason—the accidents of origin sometimes account for the anomalies of development. Hence, it is refreshing to find that

Morris Copeland shares it, for he is one of the important members of that school.

In our day, health care is one of the burgeoning industries, providing services demanded in ever-greater quantity and level of sophistication by more and more people. We think of this as a wholly new phenomenon; in our grandparents' day, a hospital was a place where, if one went at all, one went to die. Professor Copeland finds the origins of the health care industry, an industry, in ancient times, which also had its hospitals, though they had other names. The formal training of physicians began then, too, and though scholastic settings were sometimes employed, their education was essentially through the apprenticeship system, which survived into the last century.

Among the other fascinating studies in this collection of essays is an investigation of two nonpecuniary civilizations, the old kingdom in Egypt and the Inca Empire. Money and monetary transactions are so much woven into the warp and woof of our civilization that we tend to regard them as essentials of all civilization. We tend to think that the only nonpecuniary civilizations are the most primitive cultures discovered by the social anthropologists. But, as Professor Copeland shows, these two great civilizations, one of them the basis for a greater one, and the other that perished in the jungles of Middle America, managed without monetary institutions. Indeed we often forget that within our money-oriented culture, there is another nonpecuniary culture that once had a viable economy based on subsistence agriculture. By the study of nonpecuniary civilizations we can appreciate better the good and the harm our own monetary institutions are responsible for.

A feature of institutionalism in our day has been its concern with technology, which consists (from one aspect), as Clarence Ayres once wrote, of inventions and discoveries that, in turn, resulted from the combining of hitherto separate tools, instruments, materials and the like. Professor Copeland intrigues us with an account of how military technology, time after time, altered the course of history in ancient times. Another feature has been his interest in the money economy as distinct from the goods and services producing economy. We take check debits to depositors' accounts—bank deposit money—as a matter of course, and we should, considering the long history of the device. Professor Copeland traces that history back to 250 B.C.

As Professor Copeland demonstrates, the archaeologist, the paleographer and the linguist, among other specialists, have a wealth of material of interest to the student of economics. For the economy has a history and a prehistory that help to illuminate economic theory. And no one is better equipped to make that demonstration than Morris A. Copeland. Born in Rochester, N.Y., he was graduated from Amherst College and took his Ph.D. at the University of Chicago—which William Rainey Harper had turned into a beehive of research and a maternity ward of scholars a generation before—in 1921. He joined the faculty of Cornell University in that year, achieving full professorship by 1928. After service at the Federal Reserve Board, he was one of the top economists drafted into the Federal Government by the New Deal administration during the Great Depression. He served from 1933 to 1944 as executive secretary of the Central Statistical Board—a time of revolutionary advance in the collection and processing of economic statistics by the central government—then as director of research of the Bureau of the Budget and, through the periods of rearmament and the Second World War, as chief of the munitions branch of the famed War Production Board.

From 1944 to 1959, he was a member of the staff of the National Bureau of Economic Research, at a time when that top research agency was engaged in its pioneering work in developing quantitative measures of the national economy. There he undertook the research that resulted in moneyflows accounting. This is a system that complemented the national product accounts and rounded out our country's system of social accounts, the way in which our country, and now most of the countries of the world, measure economic activity and monitor the performance of their economies.

Dr. Copeland reported on his work to the American Economic Association (which he has also served as president) in 1947 and, in a full length book that is one of the classics of economics, in 1952. Just as the work of von Neumann and Morgenstern on game theory had done earlier, his book spawned shelves of studies enriching the literature of economics and finance. Moreover, from his empirical studies, he derived ideas that have become accepted theories in monetary economics. His work, as was pointed out by Jacob Cohen in a comprehensive review of this aspect of it recently, not only made a major methodological contribution but a substantial contribution to the corpus of monetary theory.

He resumed his professorship at Cornell in 1949 and eight years later became the occupant of the Robert J. Thorne chair there in his specialty, serving until retirement from the Cornell faculty. Later, he taught at the University of Missouri and the State University of New York at Albany. He has published a succession of books and articles in scientific journals.

Veblen had a theory that a social scientist's comprehension of the real world about him depended on his mind-set, his intellectual and philosophical orientation, which is a product of his life experience. Professor Copeland's experience as a teacher, a research scholar, and as an economic agency head has enabled him to achieve an understanding of what went on in the economies of ancient times from the fragments of information available from artifacts, inscriptions and relics beyond what predecessors had been able to reconstruct. One hopes he will continue to pursue his pioneering work in this fertile field, not only because the results are needed but because his example of interdisciplinary research may inspire other scholars to follow his lead.

Will Lissner
Editor-in-chief
American Journal of Economics and Sociology

ESSAYS IN
SOCIOECONOMIC EVOLUTION

Chapter I

The Evolutionary Process

Our present economy is a product of socioeconomic evolution; that is to say, it is a stage in an evolutionary process by which changes in our economic organization have come about that this process has reached in 1978. There is every reason to think that this process of change will continue into the indefinite future.

We propose to examine it in some detail. Socioeconomic evolution is in one way like the process of organic evolution that has resulted in originating various species of plants and animals. It is largely, but not quite perfectly, continuous. Between any two successive stages in an organic evolutionary sequence, there are ordinarily intermediate types of plant or animal, but occasionally, there is a jump in the process, a mutation. Similarly in the socioeconomic evolutionary process by which an economy such as ours has developed, there are ordinarily, between any two stages in its development, intermediate stages; but occasionally, there are jumps. Usually a jump in the socioeconomic evolutionary process seems to have involved a technological innovation. A major technological innovation in man's early history was learning to make a fire.

The evolutionary process that has resulted in originating the various species of plants and animals involves what is called natural selection and the survival of those fittest to

1

survive. There seems to be nothing in the socioeconomic evolutionary process that corresponds to natural selection. It is true various institutions have come into being at some time and place and ceased to exist at some later time. Thus the cult of Asclepius was important in the Greek world during the fifth, fourth, and third centuries B.C. and disappeared some time during the second. But the rise and disappearance of this institution are simply phases of the socioeconomic evolutionary process.

To understand how an economy such as ours, or such as that of the Incas in the fifteenth century A.D., has come into being, it is necessary to analyze the evolutionary process into its components, to consider the states through which the various social and economic institutions that organize economic activity have passed.

An institution such as the English language is a very complicated set of vocal and mental behavior patterns common to the people in a wide area, patterns that are prescribed by effective social sanctions. The institutions that organize our economic activity are rather less intricate and involved behavior forms than our language, but each of them is a pretty complex affair. We shall be most concerned with four institutions: property, contract, the price system, and the wage system.

Property involves personal relationships. Most of what needs to be said about property is obvious. Much of it in our present economy is private; the person who owns it has the right to do anything he wishes to do with it, provided he does not use it in a way that interferes with the rights of others. One may own a physical object, for example, a house or an article of clothing; and there are various intangibles that one may own, for example, a government bond, a share of stock in a business corporation. Some property is public; some branch of government, federal, state, or local, owns it, and some government official is in a position to say how it is to be used.

A contract is an agreement between two parties, the terms of which are, under our present law, legally binding. There is freedom of contract today in the sense any two parties are free to enter into legally binding agreements with each other that obligate each of them to do something, almost anything that is lawful. Any mentally competent adult person may be a party to a contract. Any private business corporation or partnership or any branch or agency of government may be a party to a contract, although in this case, there may be legal restrictions on the type of contract the party may enter into. A lawful contract is enforceable in the sense that if either party fails to carry out his obligations under it, the other party can obtain a legal order of enforcement. In such a case the court may, if the order is not obeyed, order a money payment of damages.

The freedom of contract we have today is a relatively recent development. What has been said above relates to the institution of contract as it now exists in the United States. This institution has quite a history. It has taken a variety of forms at various times and places. Some form of contract has been an important influence on the way business has been conducted for a very long time.

The price system puts a money value or price on each of a great variety of things, household goods, damages to one's person or property, a bribe, a tax, and so on. We consider all of these money values to be prices. All of the prices of all things priced constitute the price system. It is a system because prices seem to vary in a systematic way. This is clearly the case during what we call a business cycle or a period of inflation. The price system apparently originated in ancient Sumer in Mesopotamia some time before 3000 B.C. The number of things priced has gradually increased.

The wage system involves a relation between an employer and an employee. It puts the employer in a position to order the employee to do for him things he wants done; it imposes on the employee an obligation to do what the employer orders him to do. By its very nature it restricts the personal liberty of the employee. It may be said to be inherently undemocratic; the employer is the superior of the employee.

The wage system makes large-scale organizations possible,

business enterprises and other undertakings each of which has many employees; it puts the management in the position of being the manager of the operations of the large-scale organization. The management may be a sole proprietor of a business enterprise. But the wage system, or perhaps we should call this form of it the salary system, makes possible a more complicated type of management, a general manager and his hired subordinates, perhaps a general manager, his hired subordinates, and their hired subsubordinates.

Because of its nature, the development of the wage system has involved serious problems in connection with its impacts on the personal liberties of employees. We shall not attempt to list the resulting difficulties and evils. It will suffice to note that the employment contract is now subject to various developments that do much to protect and promote the welfare of employees. Among these developments are: collective bargaining agreements that govern many wage contracts, the social security system, the bankruptcy law, and the abolition of slavery and imprisonment for debt.

Let us consider briefly one little segment of the process of socioeconomic evolution; let us note what has happened during the last one hundred or more years in the United States to each of the four institutions on which we have chosen to focus our attention.

During the past 150 years the business corporation, and with it the property such corporations hold, has largely come into being. During this period there have been important changes in the legal system. Court decisions have done much to define the property rights business corporations have and the rights they do not have. They once claimed the right to make wage bargains with their employees that minimum wage legislation now prevents.

A person has more freedom today to make a will to determine who is to inherit any real property he possesses than was the case 150 years ago. One form of property that no longer exists is slaves.

What has been said above about freedom of contract should

be qualified to note that even today there are some restrictions on this freedom. Thus a woman has a prejudice to overcome if she wishes to enter an occupation for which women have been considered unsuitable, for example, if she wishes to become a priest or even a banker. There are still restrictions, too, in connection with positions for which only persons of high social standing have been thought suitable. But in general, most of the former restrictions based on sex, social position, or the previous condition or the then present condition of servitude have ceased to exist.

There have been various changes between, say, 1860 and 1978 in what is considered to be a lawful contract. Some of these represent attempts to broaden the definition of business practices that are regarded as imposing monopolistic restrictions on freedom of competition. Many of the changes in what constitutes a lawful contract, however, are results of what is called social legislation, legislation aimed at protecting and promoting the welfare of employees. The imposition of a legal minimum for wages has just been mentioned.

The price system has been changed by developments in the markets for goods and services and for labor. Since the 1930s collective bargaining agreements have come to play an important part in fixing the terms on which laborers are hired. Since the 1930s, too, government price support programs for various agricultural products have become a major influence in the markets for these products. And largely during the last thirty or forty years, what are called administered prices have come to be the prices at which a great many goods and services are sold. Branded goods of the sort we have today are only about one hundred years old; all branded goods are sold at administered prices. Doctors, lawyers, and several other types of professional persons fix the fees they charge; this form of administered price has been with us somewhat more than a century. A more recently developed form is the list price at which grocers and various other retailers sell the things they sell.

Before World War II, prices could be expected to rise during a cyclical upswing of business and to fall during a cyclical downswing. Since World War II, we can still expect prices to rise during an upswing; but during business recessions, price decreases, if any, have been quite small. We attribute this change in the price system to the development of collective bargaining in labor markets, of price support programs for farm products, and of administered prices for many goods and services.

The wage system has been somewhat changed by social legislation. Before the 1930s, labor unions had little influence. In general, an employer made a separate bargain with each employee. He determined the wage he offered and fixed the working conditions under which his employees had to work. Before the 1920s and 1930s, employees were not compensated for any industrial accidents they might suffer; and some forms of employment involved exposure to an industrial disease. A worker often had to choose between accepting the terms an employer offered and being unemployed. Since that time various laws have been enacted to provide compensation for industrial accidents, to promote good working conditions, and to prohibit employments causing industrial diseases. And the Norris-LaGuardia Act, passed in 1932, greatly restricted the use of injunctions against labor in industrial disputes; and the Wagner Act, passed in 1935, made clear the right of employees to organize trade unions. Following these two acts, collective bargaining developed in a good many industries. The Fair Labor Standards Act, 1938, established a minimum wage for all employees engaged in interstate commerce. The minimum was low, forty cents an hour shortly after 1938; it was too low to have much effect. It was increased to seventy-five cents an hour in 1949 and to $1.00 an hour in 1955. It did not cover agricultural workers and those processing farm products and employees in small establishments.

These brief comments on the changes during the past hundred or more years in the four institutions on which we have decided to focus our attention are, of course, by no means a complete account of the segment of the socioeconomic evolutionary process that has taken place in the United States in that period. A more complete account would include comments on what happened to other social and economic institutions; but we may note that our comments on these four imply comments on free enterprise, competition, and the business corporation.

We should probably add for the corporation that extensive trading in corporation stocks developed during the nineteenth century, that there was a stock market crash in 1929, followed by statutory regulation of trading on a margin aimed at avoiding another crash, and that financing corporations by stock issue led to the development of business practices known as "high finance" on which various restrictions have now been imposed.

Probably we should add, too, that before the middle of the nineteenth century, competition between business enterprises was almost entirely competition between small-scale undertakings, sole proprietors and partnerships. Today, it is quite largely competition between large-scale incorporated business enterprises, and, in some markets, the freedom of competition is somewhat restricted.

Before the Industrial Revolution, the profit system was an arrangement under which the sole proprietor of a business managed it in such a way as to maximize the amount by which the revenues it yielded exceeded the expenses or costs of operating it. Similarly, in the case of a partnership, the partners cooperated with each other to maximize the excess of revenues over costs. In so far as maximizing the excess of revenues over costs or profits meant maximizing what the business contributed to the gross domestic product, the profit system was an ingenious device for promoting the common welfare.

What became of this device when corporations became the owners of businesses is decidedly uncertain. In some corporations, it survived nearly intact; in others, very little was left of it. The manager or managers of a business corporation receive not the profit the corporation makes but a salary or salaries. Probably it is fair to say that with the changes that have taken place in the legal system, many business corporations, operating to maximize their profits, have become moderately satisfactory public service undertakings.

7

Chapter II

Concerning the Origin of a Money Economy

THE QUESTION, "How did a money economy such as ours ever come into being?" has sometimes been answered hypothetically in terms of an imagined previous barter economy out of which a money economy is assumed to have developed, a postulated local community in which there were a number of different types of craftsmen, each trading his product for the products of others. The advantages of adopting a medium of exchange and a standard of value in exchange in such a postulated situation have often been pointed out. While an explanation along these lines of the way a money economy originated seems to persist, there is perhaps no recent economic text that espouses it. It involves too many difficult questions about where and when there could have been such a premoney economy and whether it is likely that there ever was one.

This approaches the problem by inquiring into the way a money economy originated historically, or, more precisely, historically and prehistorically, since the inquiry necessarily takes us into prehistory.*

*The writer gratefully acknowledges the helpful comments on an earlier version of this paper made by Erle Leichty, professor of Assyriology, University Museum, University of Pennsylvania.

I

The evidence at present available indicates that a money economy first developed in Mesopotamia and that this development took place sometime before 2500 B.C. There seems to have been no such development elsewhere before 2200 B.C.[1] As a start toward answering the question, "How did it come into being in Mesopotamia?" we offer what may be called cultural snapshots of two periods, the early Ubaid period, probably sometime around the end of the fifth millennium B.C., and Sumer in the period 2500–2000 B.C. In the former period, there was no money economy; in the latter, there were money economies.

This may fairly be said to be the scientific way to deal with the question about the origin of a money economy. It is what Henri Bergson characterized as the cinematographic way. And our cultural snapshots of the two periods provide only a partial answer. A full answer would require a consideration of intermediate stages in the development process and of how one stage came to lead to another. Our cultural snapshots are only a first step toward an answer; but it is an important step. If we do not offer a cultural snapshot for any intermediate stage, it is because we do not have the necessary information.

What we say below about the early Ubaid period is based mainly on archeological findings for this and earlier periods and on the assumption that many culture traits of one period are, in large part, passed on to the next. We also draw inferences about the Ubaid period from what we know about later developments in Mesopotamia. For the Sumerian period, our main reliance is on the findings by Sumerologists of what is recorded in cuneiform script on clay tablets. But there are archeological findings about the Sumerians, too.

Our two-stage approach to the question of how a money economy came into being in Mesopotamia has been dictated by the information available and the lack of it. We can cite a

9

good deal in the way of empirical support for what we say about the early Ubaid period, although we have had to rely to some extent on inferences also. For the Sumerian period, we can document our statements much more adequately. It would not be possible today to present a comparably supported specification of any intermediate stage in the development of a money economy in Mesopotamia. There is almost no basis for determining the sequence of developments. About this, we can only guess. Very tentatively we offer a five-step guess.

Before we present our two-stage cultural snapshots, a brief note on culture periods and geography seems called for. The Sumerians lived in the part of Mesopotamia (present-day Iraq) that is south and east of Babylon. The Ubaidians lived in this area and also in the northern and western part of Mesopotamia.[2] They were preceded by the Halafians in the northern and western part and perhaps in a larger area.[3] Before the Sumerians took over the lower part of Mesopotamia in the Protoliterate or Jamdat Nasr period, the Ubaid period was followed by the Warka or Uruk period.[4]

It will be convenient to present two separate cultural snapshots for the early Ubaid period. One of them assumes that people were living in villages and relates to a typical village. The other is concerned with intervillage or intercommunity trade in an area probably wider than the Fertile Crescent. For the Sumerian period, a single cultural snapshot will be offered.

II

Cultural Snapshot I: The Village State in the Early Ubaid Period—An Hypothesis

In Mesopotamia during the early Ubaid period, each village was a politically independent entity.[5] The typical village probably had a population of no more than eight hundred and very possibly covered no more than twelve acres.[6] It was ruled by the chief priest of the village temple, who was called an ensi. He was regarded locally as the vicar of the village's tutelary deity.[7] Each temple apparently had several rooms.[8] The temple property presumably included cultivated fields, vegetable gardens, and livestock,[9] and the irrigation system.[10] It seems probable that date palms were already being cultivated at this time either in groves or as single trees. If a village had a grove, the ensi very likely owned it.[11]

The early Ubaid period was, for the most part, peaceful.[12] The typical village may well have been unfortified.[13] The only kinds of weapons that have thus far been found in the tells for this and the immeditely preceding Halaf period are stone arrowheads, clay and stone sling pellets, and stone maceheads.[14] We guess that the total population of Mesopotamia at this time may have been between a million and a little over two million.[15]

Except for the temple household of which the ensi was pater familias, the population of each village consisted of private citizens. They lived in rectangular mud brick houses or else in houses made by stretching reed matting between wooden poles.[16] Many of them owned fields on which they raised barley[17] and gardens in which they grew onions, lentils, peas and other vegetables.[18] Many of them raised cattle, sheep, pigs and goats and had shepherd dogs.[19] They may have raised ducks, also.[20] Probably, they had to do corvee work for the ensi—temple construction, construction and upkeep on the irrigation system, and cultivation of the temple fields.[21] The temple must have made available to them water for personal use and for irrigation.

Ubaidian technology at this time included the spinning and weaving of wool and of goats' hair and probably of flax fibers,[22] oil process tanning,[23] pottery making,[24] basketry,[25] and bread baking.[26] Each village not only produced a good deal of food—barley flour, garden vegetables, meats, and quite possibly dates—but it supplemented what was produced by fishing, hunting and collecting wild plant seeds. The Ubaidians

11

may well have been somewhat better provided with food than any of their contemporaries in the Near East.[27] People probably had woolen and leather clothing and footwear. There were stamp seals that presumably indicated ownership.[28] There were some metal products, though not many of them.[29] Apparently people played some kind of game; what are thought to be clay game pieces have been found at Gawra.[30] V. Gordon Childe did not consider the Ubaidians civilized; but in terms of present-day European and American standards, they may quite possibly have been better fed, housed, and clothed than a number of million people are today.

III

Cultural Snapshot II: Intercommunity Trade During the Early Ubaid Period—An Hypothesis

Even before the middle of the fifth millennium B.C., commodities were somehow moving from one community to another over a wide area.[31] This area included not only Mesopotamia, Palestine, and the rest of the Fertile Crescent, but also adjacent territory in Iraq, Iran, and Arabia. It may have included Egypt, some of modern Turkey, and the Indus Valley.[32] Among the commodities moving into Mesopotamian villages were: carnelian, obsidian, turquoise, amethyst, lapis lazuli, ivory, shells, and amazonite beads. There were also Ubaidian finds of various stone objects and a few metal objects made from materials that must have come from a number of places. Furthermore, it is clear that a considerable volume of lumber—posts, poles, and planks—must have been imported into Mesopotamia.

The fact that the commodities were moved from a considerable number of different places to various villages in Mesopotamia raises the interesting questions: Who transported them? Why was the transportation undertaken? Were there exports from Mesopotamian villages as well as imports into them?

Before attempting to answer them, let us note two characerisitcs of the intercommunity commodity movements. First, the commodities transported were, with the exception of the lumber, for the most part light and easy to carry. And in the case of lumber, a special expedition may have been required to bring it into a Mesopotamian village. If later practice may be taken as a guide, the lumber was presumably made into a raft near the forest it came from, floated down the river to the importing village and disassembled on arrival. The second characteristic of the intercommunity commodity movements other than lumber into Mesopotamia, as their nature suggests, is that the physical volume may well have been extremely small, quite possibly not much more than a few hundred pounds per year on the average.

Next, we offer a negative point about why the commodity movements took place. They presumably were not induced by the exertion of military force. The Halaf period and the Ubaid period and probably a considerable period that preceded them were comparatively peaceful. For a long time before man had metal weapons in Mesopotamia, he was probably better equipped for defense than for offense.

For light on our three questions, one might look to the findings in regard to movements of commodities between non-money communities in modern times by anthropologists who have studied them. One might also consider what anthropologists have been able to learn about such commodity movements from historical records. Herskovits (1952) reports on a large number and a great variety of cases of ceremonial exchange, barter, and trade between nonliterate communities. However, it is not clear that any one of these cases sufficiently resembles the one we are here concerned with to provide much help. We know that Mesopotamian villages had imports. The evidence to date on exports is extremely scanty. Another peculiarity of the case we are considering is the number of different source places from which the imports came and the number of village destinations.[33]

The case reported by Herskovits (1952) that most closely resembles the one with which we are here concerned is that of the Australian aborigines (pp. 200–203). The area covered by their trade routes is certainly comparable to that covered by the intercommunity trade in the Near East in the early Ubaid period. We assume that the commodity movements we are concerned with result from the activities of traders.[34] We propose to call them itinerant traders because of the wide area covered by their trading. They must commonly have acquired the commodities they transported by giving things in return and must have expected before they transported them that they could barter them to advantage in Mesopotamia. We suspect that these itinerant traders, in the means of travel they employed, enjoyed a substantial advantage over the Australian aborigines. Probably when they traveled by water they used small boats made of reeds covered with skins that were propelled by paddles.[35] The Australian aborigines apparently traveled on foot.

We incline to suppose that the itinerant traders of the early Ubaid period carried other commodities in addition to those mentioned above, among them probably salt, perfumes, and spices. And when they visited a Mesopotamian village, they presumably received food, textiles, and leather products in return for the things they brought.

There were probably not many itinerant traders. Unless they had other means of livelihood, there may not have been either in the Halaf or in the early Ubaid period enough trade to support more than one or two trading families at any one time. Probably the traders fished, hunted, and collected wild plant foods. Quite possibly they may have been itinerant minstrels as well as traders. And there seems to be no reason to think that they did not sometimes engage in robbery or piracy. Their dwellings may have been tents that they could move from place to place.

Very possibly the principal customers of the itinerant traders in the Mesopotamian villages were the ensis.

14

IV

Cultural Snapshot III: Sumerian Economies, 2500–2000 B.C.

In lower Mesopotamia, c. 2500 B.C., there were a number of city-states. Each of them was ruled by a kind of king, in most cases a ruler who was called an ensi. Frequently the ensi of a city claimed that he was acting under orders from the city's local tutelary deity when promulgating a decree[36] or engaging in some public construction work such as the building of a temple.[37] But usually he was not a priest.[38] In general, by 2500 B.C., each ensi was independent of any temple in his city. Indeed some ensis were apparently in a position to appropriate temple property.[39]

Between 2500 and 2000 B.C., for much of the time, one city-state or another in southern Mesopotamia had a sufficiently powerful military establishment to be dominant in Sumer. When this was the case, the ensis of other city-states became more or less loyal vassals to a king, who was thus at least nominally the ruler of a considerable area. At various times each of several city-states dominated Sumer. But there were times also when no city-state was dominant and when Sumer was invaded by illiterate hill people from the north. And about 2300 B.C. a foreigner, an Akkadian who came to be known as Sargon the Great, founded a dynasty that reigned for over 115 years. By conquest Sargon built up an empire that included much of the Fertile Crescent and Elam.[40]

By 2000 B.C. there were quite possibly half a dozen or more city-states, each with a population of rather more than thirty thousand.[41]

In 2000 B.C., very likely even in 2500 B.C., each Sumerian city-state was a separate money economy. It exported agricultural products and textiles and other manufactures[42] and imported raw materials, lumber, stone, metals and bitumen, and various other commodities.[43] Most imports came from and most exports went to places outside of Mesopotamia. Silver had come to serve as the principal standard of value; coinage had not yet

15

been developed; there were sixty shekels to one mina.[44] Weight and tale settlements were made in silver and in several other commodities.[45] There were recorded sales of various properties.[46] Reform edicts issued by Ur-Nammu, who became king of Ur c. 2112 B.C., were said to provide for "honest and unchangeable" weights and measures.[47] Immediately after the destruction of Agade (not long after 2200 B.C.) there seem to have been somewhat distorted price relationships.[48] At least by c. 2350 B.C., there was lending and borrowing, and apparently there were contracts at compound interest.[49] And there was imprisonment for debt defaults.[50]

Probably even before 2500 B.C., the division of labor in Sumer had progressed to the point where there were a considerable number of specialist occupations in the sense that to each occupation there were persons who devoted a major part of their working time. There were various types of handicraftsmen including smiths, carpenters, masons, jewelers, sculptors, lapidaries, potters and leather workers.[51] Also there were ensis, scribes,[52] priests, temple administrators,[53] teachers,[54] physicians,[55] and tavern keepers.[56] And of course, there were traders[57] and farmers.[58]

It seems likely that even in 2000 B.C., the individual private household made many of the manufactured goods it needed, textile and leather products, wood products and pottery. But there was a good deal of manufacturing on a business basis, too, particularly manufacturing for export. Woolen textiles were undoubtedly the most important export for Ur,[59] and probably for other cities as well. Various nontextile products must also have been manufactured for export. It seems reasonable to suppose that there was a good deal of pottery produced for sale outside of Sumer. Potter's clay was perhaps the only manufacturing raw material that Sumer was well supplied with. Quite possibly among the important exports were metal tools, weapons and utensils. Certainly for a long time, Sumer excelled in this kind of manufacture.[60] Another commodity that may well have been produced for export is perfumery.[61]

There must have been a number of different kinds of busi-

16

ness enterprises in Sumer in 2000 B.C. Presumably, traders, farmers, scribes, physicians and tavern keepers were in business for themselves, and there were doubtless brothels.[62] Interestingly, Kramer (1963) gives more information about the income account of a school for scribes, *edubba*—there were a number of them—than for any other enterprise. Tuition was the principal form of revenue: teachers' salaries the principal expense. Presumably the headmaster, *ummia,* was an entrepreneur.[63] While a great many workers were undoubtedly temple employees, there must also have been a considerable number of craftsmen and others who were in business for themselves. Roux (1966) has imagined the various shops in Ur, presumably during the Third Dynasty, c. 2112–2004 B.C. He suggests: food stores, tailors, rug makers, potters, spice vendors, perfumers, smiths, and a kind of restaurant.[64]

The temple was not only a religious institution; it was also a very large-scale business.[65] And the variety of its business operations, textile and other manufacturing, farming, date cultivation, and possibly brewing beer, would seem to make it a conglomerate.[66] However, it should be noted that there were probably some cities in which the ensi as well as the temple was in the manufacturing business. If weapons and other copper products were exported, the work of producing them was probably done by coppersmiths who were working as employees. If so, the local ensi was presumably their employer.

A good deal can be inferred about the technological know-how and related cultural attainments of the Sumerians from what has been said in Cultural Snapshots I and II. Their cultural inheritance from the Ubaid period was substantial. There were additions to the list of domesticated animals between the early Ubaid period and 2000 B.C. The most important was the horse.[67] And major improvements had been made in building-construction techniques, among them the arch, vault, and dome and the baking of bricks.[68] People had also learned how to dig canals, build dams, and store water in reservoirs.[69] Furthermore, the cuneiform system of writing developed out of a protoliterate pictographic form.[70] And with writing and money economies came number notation and arithmetic.[71]

17

Perhaps the most significant technological developments between the early Ubaid period and 2500 B.C. were the developments in metallurgy. These provided a great variety of copper and copper alloy products—utensils, tools, implements, and weapons.[72] Also there were rings, wires, and other articles made of silver and gold.[73] Among the copper and bronze products were various woodworking tools, chisels, knives, saws, etc.[74] There were also such important implements as the shovel, pickax and plow.[75]

Of outstanding significance was the impact of the development of copper and bronze products on the technology of warfare. These products included particularly effective weapons and various other types of military equipment, among them the chariot. And with them came a major development in military tactics, the phalanx formation for heavily armed infantry.[76] The consequences for Sumer and for Babylonia and Assyria as well were almost continuous struggles for empire supremacy, one city-state and then one empire after another rising to power for a time and then presently being overthrown by another that had become more powerful.

V

Concluding Comments

THE TWO CULTURAL SNAPSHOTS for the early Ubaid period are labeled hypotheses because the facts have been supplemented by inferred possibilities. A good deal less of this sort of supplement has been added in the snapshot for Sumer some two thousand years later.

We take the term, money economy, to refer to a community or a wider area in which some economic good is accepted as a standard of value, in which there are purchase and sale transactions and lending and borrowing transactions that involve payment of amounts stated in units of this standard good, and in which there are accepted ways of settling these obligations.

18

In this sense, between 2500 and 2000 B.C., each of a number of Sumerian city-states had an economy that was clearly a money economy. Equally clearly, if Cultural Snapshot I is approximately correct, in the early Ubaid period, no Mesopotamian village described by it was a money economy. And if Cultural Snapshot II is approximately correct and a much wider area such as the whole of the Fertile Crescent is regarded as an economy, it was not a money economy in this period.

Evidently, between the early Ubaid period and 2500 B.C. what we consider to be a money economy developed in Mesopotamia. Neither written records nor archeological findings enable us to say anything about the order of events in the process by which a money economy evolved. We can only guess at that. But it may help to bring out the significance of our before-and-after cultural snapshots if we venture an extremely tentative guess. It seems reasonable to suppose that the sequence may have been somewhat as follows:

I. There was, perhaps during the later Ubaid period, a substantial increase in the volume of goods imported into and exported from various communities in southern Mesopotamia. With this increase, the ensi in each community may presently have found it convenient to value each item of his external trade as equal to so many minas and shekels of silver and also to have a settlement for an export balance in the other items of his external trade made in minas of silver.[77] These developments would have meant that, for a community's exports and imports, a price system had come into being.

II. In the course of time, quite possibly even before the protoliterate period, as temple record-keeping became an established practice and as ensis came to take pride in the size of their inventories, they may have begun to figure the size of an inventory by computing the number of minas and shekels of silver that would have an equal value in exchange.[78] Thus silver may have become a standard of value for inventories as well as for external trade.

III. Beginning perhaps sometime during the Uruk period, the ensis of several southern Mesopotamian communities un-

19

dertook major programs of public works—construction and improvement and decoration of temples and extensions of irrigation systems.[79] These programs called for workers who would specialize in various crafts as masons, smiths, sculptors, etc. Probably in this way, a somewhat extensive division of labor developed. Perhaps in order to get the work done, a wage system was devised, an incentive arrangement that proved more effective than the corvee. Under this arrangement, a wage was stated as having the value of so many shekels of silver, but for a considerable period the silver value was perhaps largely a matter of kudos, the wage payment at that time being almost always made in kind. Also, if an employee occasionally received a silver ring or medal as part of his wage, he must have wanted it merely as a keepsake.

IV. Once there was a fairly extensive division of labor, it could not have taken a craftsman long to realize that he could make things for his own use. Presently, too, we assume he discovered that he could make things he could swap with fellow townsmen to get other kinds of things he wanted. Perhaps about the same time, perhaps a little later, the practice developed of valuing a craftsman's products as his wages were valued in shekels of silver and of accepting in exchange for a product either articles of silver of appropriate weight or an amount of some other widely desired good such as copper or barley having an equal value in exchange.[80] The advantage of this kind of trading was that it did not require "a double coincidence of wants," only that the payment must be in a form acceptable to the seller. And as it became more common, it must have made it easier for a handicraftsman to stop working as a temple employee and go into business on his own account. It seems reasonable to suppose that a price system for articles that were manufactured for sale originated in this way, and that the range of articles traded increased gradually. By 2700 B.C., there were sales of fields, houses, and slaves.[81]

V. Once silver had become a fairly widely accepted standard of value for wage payments and for buying and selling transactions in towns in southern Mesopotamia, the development of lending and borrowing and loan repayment transactions must have been a comparatively short next step.

Of course, this five-stage sequence is a pure guess. And the hypothetical account of the process of evolution of a money economy it provides, if it were to be truly adequate, would need substantial supplement. Between the early Ubaid period and 2500 B.C., villages became cities, ensis who were not priests took over major government functions, and war and defense activities came to absorb a great many man-hours of effort. But so far as it goes, this hypothetical five-stage sequence provides connecting links between the cultural snapshots for the early Ubaid period and the snapshot for Sumer perhaps two thousand years later.

Notes

1. A money economy may possibly have developed in the Indus Valley between 2100 and 1800 B.C. See Bridget and Raymond Allchin, *The Birth of Indian Civilization* (Baltimore: Penguin Books, 1968), especially pp. 143, 268–71, 322–23. One may be quite confident that there was no development of a money economy either in Egypt or in China before 2500 B.C. John A. Wilson, in *The Culture of Ancient Egypt* (Chicago: University of Chicago Press, 1951),p. 82, characterizes the period of the Old Kingdom in Egypt, 2700–2200, as "an age of barter." Chester G. Starr says of China, in the third or possibly the second millennium B.C., that it "came later to a civilized level and lagged behind the Near East in many respects." See *A History of the Ancient World* (New York: Oxford University Press, 1965), p. 114.
2. Ann Louise Perkins, *The Comparative Archelogy of Early Mesopotamia* (Chicago: University of Chicago Press, 1949), chap. 2, especially pp. 16, 43–45; chap. 3, especially p. 96. See also Georges Roux, *Ancient Iraq* (Harmondsworth, Middlesex, England: Penguin Books, 1966), pp. 67–68. And James Mellaart, *Early Civilizations in the Near East* (New York: McGraw-Hill Book Co., 1965), p. 68, gives a date of c. 5000 B.C. for pottery, presumably Halaf pottery, found at Eridu.
3. Perkins, *Comparative Archeology*.
4. Perkins, *Comparative Archeology*, chap. 4. M. E. I. Mallowan, *Early Mesopotamia and Iran* (New York: McGraw-Hill Book Co., 1965), p. 72, refers to the Sumerians as well established in the Jamdat Nasr period.
5. It seems clear that in Mesopotamia during the fifth millennium B.C. and a considerable part of the fourth, people lived in villages that were politically independent. Quite possibly governments that controlled more than one

21

city did not come until the early dynastic period. According to Mallowan, *Early Mesopotamia and Iran*, p. 28, this period began about 5000 B.C.

6. According to Robert J. Braidwood's article on prehistoric villages on the Kurdistan Steppe, Iraq, in the *Encyclopaedia Britannica*, 1968, vol. 2, pp. 234–37, the typical village in the Halaf period covered somewhat less than an acre and had a population of no more than five hundred. Frank C. Hole's study, "Evidences of Social Organization from Western Iran," in *New Perspectives in Archeology* (Chicago: Aldine Publishing Co., 1968), relates to villages on the Kuzistan Steppe between the Tigris River and the Zagros Mountains at three different periods. The date he gives for the last of these is c. 4000 B.C. It seems to be the early Ubaid period or possibly the late Halaf period. He thought that at this time Eridu was the largest village in Mesopotamia and that it had an area of about twenty acres. He thought no village on the Kuzistan Steppe had a population of more than eight hundred or covered an area of more than twelve acres.

7. C. Leonard Woolley, *The Sumerians* (London: Oxford University Press, 1928; reprint ed. New York: W. W. Norton and Co., 1965), p. 18. Woolley attributes the origin of a government by an ensi to the Sumerians, but it seems reasonable to suppose that it went back at least to the Ubaidians. V. Gordon Childe, *Social Evolution* (New York: Schuman, 1951), pp. 155–59, seems to imply such an arrangement during the Ubaid period.

8. Perkins, *Comparative Archeology*, pp. 65ff. and 87ff. gives descriptions of the remains of temples that have been excavated. See also Roux, *Ancient Iraq*, p. 69.

9. This was the case in Sumer perhaps 2,000 years later. It seems likely that it was then at least a 2,000-year-old arrangement.

10. Hole, "Social Organization," p. 50, says the typical village irrigation system in his third period was a simple one. See also Roux, *Ancient Iraq*, p. 71.

11. A. Leo Oppenheim, *Ancient Mesopotamia: Portrait of a Dead Civilization* (Chicago: University Press, 1964), pp. 32, 84, 312, suggests that date palms were cultivated both in groves and as individual trees well before the third millenium B.C. Cultivation requires artifical fertilization of the female tree, Samuel N. Kramer, *The Sumerians: Their History, Culture and Character* (Chicago: University of Chicago Press, 1963), p. 109.

12. Mellaart, *Early Civilizations*, p. 130, suggests that the displacement of the Halfians by the Ubaidians was a matter of economic, not military, superiority since they had few metal weapons. During Neolithic times and the Halaf and early Ubaid periods, before they had metal weapons, the people in Mesopotamia seem to have been comparatively peaceful.

13. Childe, *Social Evolution*, p. 150, indicates that the typical village was unfortified in the Halaf period. Perkins, *Comparative Archeology*, p. 41, reports a citadel wall of this period found in Tell Chaghir Bazar. But her reports on the Ubaid period include no findings of fortifications.

14. See Perkins, *Comparative Archeology*, pp. 35, 36, 61, 62, and 85 on findings of weapons for the Halaf and Ubaid periods.

15. This guess assumes an average population of 750 and that there were between 1,400 and 2,800 villages. There is no good way to determine how many villages there were. We may note that if the average village, including pasture land and cultivated fields, covered an area of about a quarter section,

probably a little less than an acre per family, this would mean that villages occupied between one and two percent of the alluvial Tigris-Euphrates plain, which was about 35,000 square miles, according to L. H. Dudley Buxton. See "Mesopotamia," *Encyclopaedia Britannica*, 1929, vol. 15, p. 288. We do not know how much of this plain was habitable. Roux, *Ancient Iraq*, p. 71, says the villages in the Ubaid period were "extremely numerous." But he makes it clear that a simple irrigation system and an embankment or levee may often have been necessary conditions for the establishment of a village. The number of villages may well have been either less than 1,400 or more than 2,800.

16. Perkins, *Comparative Archeology*, pp. 70, 88, 80; Woolley, *The Sumerians*, pp. 13, 14; Roux, *Ancient Iraq*, pp. 69, 70.

17. Woolley, *The Sumerians*, p. 14; Childe, *Social Evolution*, p. 150; Braidwood, *Encyclopaedia Britannica*, 1968, vol. 2, p. 236; Mellaart, *Early Civilizations*, p. 122; Hole, "Social Organization," p. 250. According to Oppenheim, *Ancient Mesopotamia*, p. 314, barley was preferred to wheat because it "can be grown in poor and alkaline soil."

18. Oppenheim, *Ancient Mesopotamia*, implies that onions, lentils, and various other vegetables had been domesticated long before the period with which he is mainly concerned, the second millenium B.C. See also Victor R. Boswell, "Pea," *Encyclopaedia Britannica*, 1972, vol. 16, p. 966, Victor R. Boswell and John W. Bundy,"Onion," *Encyclopaedia Britannica*, 1972, vol. 17, pp. 493–94.

19. Mellaart, *Early Civilizations*, p. 123; Childe, *Social Evolution*, p. 150; Woolley, *The Sumerians*, p. 14; Braidwood, *Encyclopaedia Britannica*, 1968, vol. 2, p. 236.

20. Mellaart, *Early Civilizations*, p. 124.

21. The ensi must have had some way to get work on the temple and the irrigation system done for him by private citizens. The corvee seems the most likely. Cf. Childe, *Social Evolution*, pp. 159, 160.

22. Woolley, *The Sumerians*, p. 15; Braidwood, *Encyclopaedia Britannica*, 1968, vol. 2, p. 236, Mellaart, *Early Civilizations*, p. 122; Hole, "Social Organization," pp. 250, 263.

23. Martin Levey, *Chemistry and Chemical Technology in Ancient Mesopotamia* (London, New York, Princeton: Elsevier Publishing Co., 1959), pp. 64, 78. Levey implies that there was tanning in the Hassunah period (this immediately preceded the Halaf period) and even earlier.

24. Woolley, *The Sumerians*, p. 15; Childe, *Social Evolution*, p. 150; Hole, "Social Organization," p. 259; Perkins, *Comparative Archeology*, pp. 46–60, 74–83. Perkins also reports finds of pottery in the Hassunah and Halaf periods. Hole says pottery was made with a potter's wheel. Perkins reports both hand-made and wheel-made pottery for the Ubaid period, pp. 50 and 83. Roux, *Ancient Iraq*, p. 69, says some pottery was made with a slow wheel.

25. Grace M. Crowfoot, "Textiles, Basketry, and Mats," in *A History of Technology*, eds. Charles Singer, E. J. Holmyard, and A. R. Hall (New York: Oxford University Press, 1954),vol. 1, p. 418; Julian H. Steward, *Theory of Cultural Change* (Normal, Ill.: University of Illinois Press, 1962), p. 201.

26. Hole, "Social Organization," p. 251. Perkins reports finds of ovens for both the Halaf and the Ubaid periods.

27. Childe, *Social Evolution*, p. 150; Roux, *Ancient Iraq*, pp. 23–24. Roux's comments refer primarily to the third millennium B.C.; but he notes that farm-

ing land was "even richer in antiquity before salinization of the soil took place" (see p. 71).

28. Perkins, *Comparative Archeology*, pp. 63, 64, 87; Hole, "Social Organization," p. 259.

29. Woolley, *The Sumerians*, p. 14. Perkins, *Comparative Archeology*, reports only a few finds of metal objects. See also Roux, *Ancient Iraq*, p. 70.

30. Perkins, *Comparative Archeology*, pp. 61, 62.

31. Childe, *Social Evolution*, pp. 151, 152, reports that shell from the Persian Gulf had been carried as far as Syria during the Halaf period; also, that obsidian from Lake Van (perhaps 400 miles north of Babylon) was found in various places in Mesopotamia. According to Mellaart, *Early Civilizations*, there was extensive trade during the Halaf period. Perkins, *Comparative Archeology*, p. 63, reports that beads of various materials that must have been transported from a number of places were found at Gawra (Ubaid level XIII): carnelian, obsidian, turquoise, amethyst, lapis lazuli, ivory, and shell. She also reports, pp. 8, 37, 65, on copper articles found in tells of the Ubaid and earlier periods. The copper may have come from Oman (Arabia) or from the Zagros Mountains. Further, she reports, pp. 8, 33–35, 62, 85, 86, finds for the Halaf and Ubaid periods of stone stamp seals, stone arrowheads and maceheads, and other stone articles. The different kinds of stone used to make these things—flint, marble. diorite, and steatite—must have been imported. Nor is this quite all; she reports occasional finds in northern Mesopotamia of stone used as special parts of buildings, such as door sills and fireplace flooring. But she characterizes these uses of stone as "very rare."

32. William C. Hayes, *Most Ancient Egypt* (Chicago: University of Chicago Press, 1965), p. 136, implies that there was trade with Egypt in the Neolithic period. Perkins, *Comparative Archeology*, p. 86, reports that two amazonite beads of the early Ubaid period were found at Ur. She suggests India as the likely source of the amazonite, as does Roux, *Ancient Iraq*, p. 71. Perkins also reports, p. 86, that a piece of gold wire was found at Ur. The nearest source for the gold was some place in Elam more than 100 miles away.

33. Melville J. Herskovits, in *Economic Anthropology* (New York: Alfred A. Knopf, Inc., 1952), reports several cases in which more than two communities were involved. For example, in the Nilgiri Hills case (India) four tribes were participants (pp. 156–159). But in general the number was small.

34. Karl Marx long ago—in *Capital* (Chicago: Charles H. Kerr & Co., 1906), vol. 1, p. 100—suggested that intercommunity trade must have developed earlier than intracommunity trade. We assume there was no intracommunity trade in a Mesopotamian village in the early Ubaid period. There were, of course, nontrade forms of exchange such as the exchange of services between husband and wife in the operation of a household.

35. This type of boat was used by the Sumerians, but it must have been developed long before the third millenium B.C. Apparently, it is still being used in Mesopotamia, cf. Kramer, *Sumerians*, p. 104. The Ubaidians seem to have had other types of boats, also. See Perkins, *Comparative Archeology*, p. 86, on the clay models that have been found. These models suggest wood construction. One of them was a model of a sailboat that had "a socket for the mast, and holes to which stays could be attached." The other principal one was a model of a flat-bottomed boat.

36. Thus, Urukagina of Lagash, claiming to have been directed to do so by Ningirsu, the city's tutelary deity, c. 2350 B.C., promulgated various edicts

24

to effect social reforms, Kramer, *Sumerians,* p. 82; Roux, *Ancient Iraq,* p. 128.
    37. For example, Lugalannemunda of Adab, Kramer, *Sumerians,* p. 51; Gudea of Lagash, Roux, *Ancient Iraq,* pp. 153-54.
    38. Only one ensi after 2500 B.C. seems to have been recorded as having been a priest. Il, the temple head of a city called Hallab, became ensi of Umma c. 2400 B.C. (Kramer, *Sumerians,* p. 57).
    39. Kramer, *Sumerians,* p. 80; Roux, *Ancient Iraq,* p. 128.
    40. The history of Sumer is outlined in Kramer, *Sumerians,* pp. 49–71 and Roux, *Ancient Iraq,* pp. 127–63. The following changes in dominance in Sumer are reported: (1) Hegemony passed from Kish to Ur, perhaps some time during the twenty-seventh century B.C., when Mesannepadda founded what is called the First Dynasty of Ur. (2) This Ur dynasty was followed by a period of confusion during at least a part of which Elamites dominated Sumer. Probably in either the twenty-sixth or the twenty-fifth century B.C., Ur-Nanshe founded a dynasty of Lagash that assumed Sumerian hegemony. (3) Although this dynasty lasted for perhaps more than a century, before it terminated there were other cities each of which for a time may have dominated Sumer—Erech and Adab, also Mari, a Semitic city located well over 250 miles up the Euphrates from Sumer. (4) The last member of the Lagash dynasty was Urukagina. From him, Sumerian hegemony passed briefly to Lugalzaggesi of Umma. (5) There followed the Akkad dynasty established by Sargon. On approximate dates for Sargon and his successors, see the table of dynasties prepared by J. A. Brinkman, which appears as an appendix to Oppenheim, *Ancient Mesopotamia,* pp. 335 ff. (6) This dynasty ended in a period of confusion dominated by a hill people, the Gutians. (7) Next, Sumerian hegemony was assumed briefly by Erech. (8) Then followed the great Third Dynasty of Ur.
    41. Kramer cuts down an estimate of the population of Ur by Woolley to about 200,000, c. 2000 B.C., and cites an estimate by I. M. Diakonoff for Lagash (presumably earlier than that) of 100,000 (*Sumerians,* pp. 88–89). Roux, *Ancient Iraq,* p. 121, notes an estimate for Lagash for sometime around 2500 or 2600 B.C. of 30,000 to 35,000. Julian H. Steward, in his *Theory of Cultural Change,* advances the hypothesis that water supply was the critical population limiting factor in Mesopotamia , and makes a strong case for this hypothesis. It seems reasonable to suppose that improved water-supply techniques involving canals, dams, and reservoirs largely account for a great population increase from the early Ubaid period to 2500 B.C. See Kramer, *Sumerians,* pp. 53–56.
    42. Woolley, *The Sumerians,* p. 49; Kramer, *Sumerians,* p. 104.
    43. Woolley, *The Sumerians,* pp. 45, 46; Kramer, *Sumerians,* p. 67; Levey, *Chemical Technology,* pp. 107, 109, 179, 196.
    44. Kramer, *Sumerians,* pp. 74, 107; Woolley, *The Sumerians* p. 117; Oppenheim, *Ancient Mesopotamia,* p. 86; Roux, *Ancient Iraq,* p. 118.
    45. Kramer, *Sumerians,* pp. 55, 74, 78, 87; Levey, *Chemical Technology,* p. 179; Oppenheim, *Ancient Mesopotamia,* p. 87.
    46. Kramer, *Sumerians,* p. 79, reports documents recording "deeds of sales" of fields, houses, and slaves beginning c. 2700 B.C. For the period of the Third Dynasty of Ur, see Roux, *Ancient Iraq,* p. 158.
    47. On the edicts of Ur-Nammu, see Kramer, *Sumerians,* p. 84; Roux, *Ancient Iraq,* p. 150. On the date, see Oppenheim, *Ancient Mesopotamia,* p. 336.
    48. Agade was a city built from scratch by Sargon the Great, Kramer,

Sumerians, p. 61. It was destroyed when one of his successors, probably his grandson, was overthrown by the Gutians. Kramer, p. 64, says that thereafter "prices were inflated"—apparently oil, grain, and wool prices—to a great extent. The name of the city can also be written "Akkade."

49. Woolley, *The Sumerians*, p. 118, reports a maximum legal interest rate of 20 percent for silver loans and one of 33 1/3 percent for loans of barley. His reference to the Third Dynasty of Ur suggests a period before 2100 B.C. for these maxima. Computation tables have been found that include exponential functions, Kramer, *Sumerians*, p. 93. According to Oppenheim, *Ancient Mesopotamia*, p. 107, these tables were used for compound interest computations. One who is accustomed to our rules that sharply define the means by which a money obligation must be paid off is apt to think of such a compound-interest contract as one that ordinarily obligates the debtor to pay his debt in minas and shekels of silver. It would probably be more nearly correct to suppose that in Sumer, in the twenty-first century B.C., a debt was hardly ever paid in this way. All that can be said is that the means of payment must be acceptable to the creditor.

50. One of Urukagina's reforms referred to above (see note 36) was the freeing of debtors he thought had been unjustly imprisoned.

51. A tablet excavated at Ur by Sir Leonard Woolley that relates to work done at a temple c. 1,975 B.C. lists the following occupations: jewelers, sculptors, lapidaries, fullers, and basket makers, Kramer, *Sumerians*, p. 101. Presumably, temple workshops also employed spinners, weavers, and dyers; and they may have employed potters, perfumers, and dye makers. Some of the dyes used in the manufacture of textiles and leather goods were probably imported. But dyes were also manufactured in Sumer. See Levey, *Chemical Technology*, chap. 8.

52. Kramer, *Sumerians*, pp. 230, 231.

53. Ibid., p. 141.

54. Ibid., p. 232.

55. Ibid., pp. 96, 98.

56. Oppenheim, *Ancient Mesopotamia*, p. 116.

57. Ibid., pp. 92, 116. He does not say much about Sumerian traders, but he says Assyrian traders in the nineteenth century B.C. moved freely from city to city and took pride in their social status. Traders were presumably concerned with imports and exports.

58. See Kramer, *Sumerians*, pp. 105–9, on the "farmers almanac." Kramer notes that since "farmers were probably illiterate this manual was presumably written for the managers of large estates."

59. Ibid., p. 104.

60. See Levey, *Chemical Technology*, pp. 197, 205, 208.

61. Ibid., p. 132.

62. Cf. Woolley, *The Sumerians*, p. 65.

63. Kramer, *Sumerians*, pp. 230–32.

64. What Roux, *Ancient Iraq*, pp. 198–199, says about the shops in Ur occurs in a chapter entitled "In the Days of Hammurabi." But the excavations by Sir Leonard Woolley on which it is based apparently revealed conditions during the Third Dynasty.

65. According to Kramer, *Sumerians*, p. 104, "thousands of tons of wool

were worked annually in Ur," presumably in the temples there.

66. Enannatum II is known chiefly for having restored "Ningirsu's beer brewery," Kramer, *Sumerians*, p. 57. Since Ningirsu was the tutelary deity of Lagash, the brewery was presumably operated by the temple.

67. Oppenheim, *Ancient Mesopotamia*, pp. 45–46.

68. Kramer, *Sumerians*, p. 4; Woolley, *The Sumerians*, p. 44. Kramer and Woolley imply that the Sumerians originated these techniques. They may have inherited them.

69. On the digging of canals, probably in the twenty-fifth century B.C., see note 41 above. This work must have involved metal digging implements. See note 72 below on metal products.

70. Kramer, *Sumerians*, pp. 302–6. The account Perkins gives of the pottery decorations and stamp seals of the Halaf, Ubaid, and Warka periods makes it clear that these people must have been on the verge of developing pictographic writing. She assumes the beginnings of pictographic writing during the Protolilterate or Jamdat Nasr period (*Comparative Archeology*, p. 199).

71. Kramer, *Sumerians*, pp. 91–93. In addition to the exponential function tables (see note 49 above), the Sumerians had quite a number of others, including multiplication tables, tables of squares and cubes and square roots, and tables of sums of squares.

72. Levey, *Chemical Technology*, pp. 196, 197; C. N. Bromehead, "Mining and Quarrying," in *A History of Technology*, eds. Charles Singer, E. J. Holmstard, and A. R. Hall (New York: Oxford University Press, 1954), vol. 1, p. 591. By 3000 B.C., copper was refined, annealed, and cast in various shapes. During the third millenium B.C., charcoal was used in the furnaces, and a bellows was used. Sometime during the latter part of it, bronze came to replace copper in many uses.

73. Levey, *Chemical Technology*, p. 179.

74. Kramer, *Sumerians*, p. 103.

75. Ibid., 106. According to Oppenheim, *Ancient Mesopotamia*, p. 314, the plow had a seeding attachment.

76. The standard of Ur found by Sir Leonard Woolley, *The Sumerians*, pp. 50–52, shows chariots and infantry in what Woolley considered to be a phalanx. A probable date for the standard is around 2500 B.C. See S. M. Cole, "Land Transport Without Wheels," in *A History of Technology*, eds. Charles Singer, E. J. Holmyard and A. R. Hall (New York:Oxford University Press, 1954), vol. 1, p. 705. By the time of Eannatum, perhaps c. 2400 B.C., there was apparently less emphasis on the chariot and an improved phalanx formation had been developed, Woolley, *The Sumerians*, pp. 55, 56.

77. The Ubaid period probably lasted some six or seven hundred years, and during this time the rate of culture change seems to have accelerated (Roux, *Ancient Iraq*, p. 72; Steward, *Cultural Change*, p. 195; Braidwood, *Encyclopaedia Britannica*, 1968, vol. 2, p. 235). We do not know that this acceleration involved a marked increase in imports into and exports from Mesopotamian communities, but it is reasonable to assume that this was the case. We follow the suggestion of Marx that the exchange of commodities developed first between communities. (See note 34 above.) We assume it was in intercommunity trade that exchange on a price-system basis first developed.

78. In historical times, as Roux, *Ancient Iraq*, pp. 124, 159, makes clear,

the Sumerians were great record keepers. We assume they inherited this propensity from their predecessors. Writing is thought to have developed to provide for temple records. The first written documents that have come down to us are temple accounts found at Erech. See Hans G. Güterbock's article, "Babylonia and Assyria: History," in the *Encyclopaedia Britannica*, 1968, vol. 2, p. 960.

79. Roux, *Ancient Iraq*, pp. 72–74; Steward, *Cultural Change*, pp. 195–97.

80. We suggest that silver initially became a standard of value for imports and exports only and that its use as a standard of value was gradually extended—in Stage II to temple inventories, in Stage III to wages, and in Stage IV to commodity purchases and sales. We assume that in none of these stages was there agreement on silver as a generally acceptable means of payment (or "medium of exchange"). There was probably—almost certainly—no such agreement in Hammurabi's day (c. 1792–1750 B.C.).

81. Kramer, *Sumerians*, p. 79.

Chapter III

The Economies of
Two Great Nonpecuniary Civilizations

We propose to study the economies of two great civilizations, that of Egypt in the days of the Old Kingdom, 2700–2200 B.C., and that of the Inca Empire, 1438–1532 A.D. We think they should be studied because each of them presents a kind of paradox.

We tend to take it for granted that an economy that has an extensive division of labor with workers engaged in producing things that are to be used by other people must be a money economy. We tend to assume that each of the things so produced must be produced for sale and that the would-be user must pay a money price for it. We are particularly likely to assume this in the case of an economy with craftsmen skilled in various crafts, an economy that manufactures textiles, metal products, and other things for persons other than those engaged in manufacturing them and that constructs great buildings that require involved enginnering planning.

Egypt had a population of about one million; the Inca Empire had a population estimated at more than ten times that. Each country had an area of some 350,000 square miles, although in the case of Egypt only a small fraction of the total area was habitable. Each country had a strong central government that kept records. In each economy, there was a fairly extensive division of labor. Although in both countries agriculture was the predominant industry, each had a manufacturing industry that produced textiles and metal products. Also, each produced great buildings that were extremely impressive engineering feats even though the builders had only very primitive construction equipment.

The paradox that each of these countries presents is that despite its division of labor, its manufacturing industries, and the impressive and nicely engineered buildings it produced, it was essentially a nonmoney economy. We shall be concerned to find out how, under these circumstances, its economic activity was organized.

I. Egypt in the Days of the Old Kingdom

The period of the Old Kingdom began c. 2700 B.C. By that time, the Egyptians had become very well satisfied with the civilization they had achieved. Their external contacts were principally with their neighbors, the peoples of Sinai on the east, of Nubia in the southeast, and of Libya in the west. All these peoples were somewhat less culturally advanced. There were contacts also with Byblos in Lebanon. They looked down on all non-Egyptians; in fact, they considered them not quite human.[1]

The population of Egypt toward the end of the Old Kingdom, c. 2200 B.C., was probably about one million. Most of the people were fellahin, farmers bound to the soil. They tilled the fields they had inherited and tended their livestock, sheep, goats, and asses, and probably some pigs. If crops were favorable—they raised mostly wheat—they had a livelihood, not much more.[2]

They were ruled by a king who was considered to be a god on earth. Until about 2500 B.C., he had only a small staff of priests and officials. During the later years of the Old Kingdom, 2500–2200 B.C., the staff was increased somewhat.[3]

In the very early days, Egypt had had the problem of draining the swamps along the Nile. By 2700 B.C., the problem had become to some extent one of providing enough water for tilling the fields. An extensive system of catch basins had been built at intervals along the Nile to catch the water when the river was high. And a great many irrigation canals had been dug. The dedication of a new catch basin or canal was an occasion during the third dynasty, 2700–2650 B.C., and doubtless before that, at which the king may have appeared in person.[4]

Egypt had no forest resources and little in the way of mineral resources of her own. She imported cedar from Lebanon on a type of vessel known as a Byblos ship. This was a square-rigged sailing vessel with a single mast. It carried a pair of oars for negotiating in a harbor. It had a crew of perhaps 120, and was about 150 feet long. We assume such ships were built at Byblos by Phoenician workmen. We do not know whether the ships that carried lumber to Egypt were owned by the king of Egypt or by Phoenicians. However, it seems likely that Phoenicians sailed such vessels to other ports on the Mediterranean. If so, the ships they sailed on were presumably owned by Phoenicians.

For transportation along the Nile there was a cruder type of vessel in use. It had a bifid mast. Byblos ships may have been used, too. All such transportation was probably a crown monopoly.[5]

The relation between Egypt and Byblos was very friendly for a considerable time. The king of Egypt sent presents to the prince who ruled the city-state of Byblos, and there were Egyptians stationed in the city who had built a temple to Re there. But about 2185 B.C., there were difficulties, and the temple was burned to the ground.[6]

Egypt imported gold, silver, copper, ivory, wine, and olive oil. To get these imports the king organized mining and trading expeditions. The men who went on one of these expeditions were fellahin conscripted for the purpose. Egypt was divided into a number of districts or nomes. The governor of each of these districts was called a nomarch. He selected the conscripts from his area, and the man to be in charge of them. Egypt did

31

not have much of a regular army; the men on one of these expeditions may not infrequently have had to fight. Egypt had gold, copper, and turquoise mines in Sinai. Various imports came by caravan, especially from Sudan and Nubia.[7]

Although Egypt was predominantly an agricultural country, she had skilled craftsmen, and she manufactured gold and silver articles, textiles, glass, and papyrus writing materials. She could use her manufactures and the wheat she raised to pay for the lumber, olive oil, and other things she imported. Her trade relations with the rest of the world were on a barter basis, and internally Egypt was pretty much a nonmoney economy.[8]

Possibly around 3400 B.C.,, there had been contacts between Egypt and Sumer in Mesopotamia. Egypt seems to have borrowed several culture traits: cylinder seals, a brickwork masonry paneling design, an artistic decorative design that pictured two fabulous and fanciful beasts, and boats of a distinctively Mesopotamian type. Quite possibly, too, the Sumerian cuneiform writing stimulated the development of hieroglyphics. But, by 2700 B.C., Egypt had developed a disinclination for foreign contacts, except for what was involved in getting her imports. At this time she was essentially ignorant of the developments of Mesopotamian civilization and its military technology.[9]

There were three forms of Egyptian script by 2700 B.C.: (1) hieroglyphs—this form was used for official documents and in literature; (2) hieratic—this form was used in business communications, also in private letters; it was cursive; (3) a religious script somewhat like the hieroglyphic. The hieroglyphic was the oldest form. It developed as a magic ceremony; putting a statement into hieroglyphs was thought to give it magic potency. Some hieroglyphs were symbols of objects; others were phonetic symbols, some of them for whole syllables, some for individual consonants.[10]

The Step Pyramid was built during the third dynasty, 2700–2650 B.C. King Djoser commissioned his vizier, Imhotep, to build it. Imhotep was an able architect engineer. He was also a priest and a particularly competent physician. After his death he was deified as the god of healing.[11]

The Great Pyramid at Gizeh was built while Khufu (or Cheops) was king. Its corners were accurately oriented, and the square that constituted its base was a practically perfect square and was almost perfectly level. It was approximately 485 feet high; each side of its square base measured nearly 756 feet. The great blocks of stone of which it was built were accurately trimmed and placed. They weighed on the average about 2 1/2 tons each. There were some 2,300,000 of them. They were brought from the quarry across the river on barges, then dragged a mile and a quarter over a causeway to the construction site. The causeway had been specially built to facilitate this haul. Even building it was a big undertaking. It was six feet wide, and it was made of polished stone.[12]

The Great Pyramid and the other two major pyramids were built and the Sphinx was carved during the fourth dynasty, 2650–2500 B.C. It seems probable that much of the work was done during the season when the Nile was high and the food stocks of the fellahin were low. Herodotus tells us that it took a hundred thousand men ten years to build the causeway, and that the Great Pyramid was twenty years in building. If a hundred thousand men were employed continuously during this period in building it, some three million man-years were spent on the whole undertaking, something like one man-year for each great block of stone.[13]

In addition to the fellahin who were conscripted for the purpose, a great many other men were needed. There were the stone masons, skilled craftsmen who trimmed the blocks of stone very precisely and fitted them nicely together. Quite possibly, too, they supervised the quarrying, and they were certainly needed for polishing the stones for the causeway. Another considerable group of men employed in building the pyramid were the professional engineering workers who took the astronomical observations and made the calculations required in planning the causeway and the pyramid. And at the top of this group and in charge of the whole undertaking was the Overseer of All Works of the King.[14]

Nearly all of the workers, including the masons and the professional staff, together with their families, seem to have been housed and otherwise provided for in a camp established for the purpose. In fact, the men and women who performed various services for these people, providing them with food and water, taking care of their quarters, washing their clothes, etc., doubtless lived in this camp, also.[15]

The mechanical equipment the Egyptians had to help them in building the pyramids and temples and other structures was exceedingly crude, just simple devices such as levers and log rollers. There were no pulleys, no wheeled vehicles, no cranes. We do not know what the barges they used to bring the great stone blocks across the river were like. One of them must have been big enough to float when a stone block was loaded on it. It may have been propelled by an oar or a paddle or perhaps a long pole. Loading a stone block on it and unloading the block were doubtless manual operations that took perhaps half a dozen men. Over the causeway a stone block was pushed or dragged along on rollers. After the first course, there was the problem of getting the blocks of stone into place. Presumably a ramp was built, possibly of gravel, up which the blocks could be pushed on rollers. More of a ramp was needed for each additional course.[16]

Not only was the mechanical equipment used in building the pyramids extremely primitive, but also only very primitive planning techniques were available. No doubt the cursive hieratic script was an important help in the planning. But the Egyptian arithmetic was almost impossibly awkward. The number system, much like that used by the Romans, did not have place-value notation, although it had a decimal base. As a result, multiplying or dividing one number by another was an extremely laborious task. Moreover, the only multiplication table the Egyptians knew was the two-times table. Also, their difficulties in making calculations were by no means helped by a curious rule that they adhered to. Every fraction except 2/3 and 3/4 had to have one as a numerator. Thus 23/24 was equal to 1/2 + 1/3 + 1/8. We shall not attempt to explain the way they multiplied one three-place number by another or how they did what we call long division. Suffice it to say that it may have taken a man, probably an assistant engineer, an hour or more to make a computation that we can make in less than a minute with a computer or a slide rule. But perhaps it should be noted that Egyptians had some knowledge of square roots and that they took 3.16 as the approximate value of pi.[17] Thus far, nothing has been said about the units the Egyptians used in making their measurements. To remedy this omission, this little table of weights and measures is added here:

Distance: *Cubit.* This unit seems to have been standardized and was equal to 20.7 inches.
         Schene. This unit was not standardized. It was probably equal to between 3 1/2 and 7 miles.
Area: *Aurure.* This was said to be equal to 67.7 hundredths of an acre.
Volume, dry: *Artaba.* This was said to be equal to 1.1 bushels.
Volume, liquid: *Hen.* Apparently equal to 1.01 pints.
Weight: *Deben.* This was apparently equal to about .206 pound avoirdupois. This unit seems to have been used chiefly for gold, silver, and copper.

To this table we should append a word about how the Egyptians measured time. Each year consisted of 365 solar days; they did not have a leap year, although they realized that there was something wrong about treating each year as having just 365 days. They divided each year into twelve months of 30 days each with 5 extra days at the end of the year. A day was divided into twenty-four hours.[18]

At this point it seems best to consider somewhat systematically the Egyptian labor force. We are accustomed to thinking of the population of a modern industrialized country as consisting of two parts, the labor force and all other people. Certainly, the institutional situation in ancient Egypt in the days of the Old Kingdom was very different from that in the

United States today. But we think it is none the less proper to divide the population of ancient Egypt as we divide ours into labor force and all others.

The fellahin who tilled the arable land and tended their livestock were a very large part of the Egyptian labor force. There were also the skilled craftsmen employed in various crafts, government officials, and the engineering staff engaged in planning the pyramids and other public buildings. All of these were government employees, and there were other government employees, too. The labor force included, also, the priests attached to the various temples and underlings that served them. Furthermore, there were the concubines and personal servants of important officials and other persons of high social status. Still another group of members of the labor force were the prostitutes.[19]

Thus far, only one type of skilled craftsmen has been noted, the stone masons. How many other types there were is not clear. There were certainly carpenters, sculptors, artists who painted pictures, and men skilled in ivory carving.[20]

Other workers included those who spun the linen and the wool thread, and wove the linen and woolen cloth, probably women, the gold and silversmiths and the coppersmiths who made various metal articles, and the men who made papyrus writing materials. Most of these workers were employed in or by government workshops; but there were temple workshops, too.[21]

One type of priests merits special attention, the priests who were physicians and surgeons. Only priests were doctors in Egypt at that time. And while for many such doctors magic incantations and appeals for supernatural help were important in the treatments they gave their patients, there were doctors, too, who treated their patients on the basis of the best scientific knowledge of medicine and surgery then available and made no attempt to seek supernatural help in the treatments they prescribed; they were extremely skilled surgeons, and they had a pharmacopoeia of several hundred medicaments. The report of one case given in what has come to be know as the Edwin

Smith Papyrus is particularly interesting. The patient had suffered a compound fracture of the skull that resulted in a partial
paralysis of one side of the body. The surgeon confessed he
could not cure this fracture. He recommended relaxation and
continued observation. The English translation of this papyrus
goes on to say of the ptient: "Thou shouldst distinguish him
from one whom something entering from outside has smitten."
Thus the papyrus report made clear that the "fracture and
partial paralysis were products of flesh and blood suffering
from a physical blow," and "not a product of divine or demoni-
acal force."[22]

Egypt during the Old Kingdom was a totalitarian state.
It was also largely a planned economy. By this is meant principally three things:

(1) The gross national product and its component parts
may be said to have been planned. It is true that neither the
king nor his vizier ever visualized all of what was to be produced in detail. Much of the national product was just the
result of having the facilities and the materials that were available pretty fully utilized. This was true of the crops that were
raised, grain, flax, and papyrus reeds. It was true, also, of the
wool and linen yarn that was spun and the cloth that was
woven; the spinners and weavers simply used the materials
that were doled out to them. The ivory carvers, metal workers,
and makers of writing materials did likewise. The wool that
was produced was the result of natural growth. The land allotments were for the most part hereditary. When the king's
waterworks produced additional land, his agents surely assigned the new plots. And the men who doled out the various
kinds of available materials in effect planned a substantial
part of the national product. Other parts were very definitely
planned, the mining and trading expeditions, the work on catch
basins and irrigation canals, and the pyramid and other construction projects.

(2) The work done by all the various members of the labor
force may be said to have been planned. For many of them of
course there were no specific job assignments. The workers

simply continued to do the kind of thing they had been doing. This was true of the fellahin, of most priests, of the concubines and personal servants, of a good many government employees, and probably of many metal workers. But the workers on mining and trading expeditions and on the various construction projects, on catch basins and irrigation canals, all had specific job assignments, as no doubt did the sculptors and picture painters.

(3) The stock of food supplies and other goods in the hands of public officials that was held in reserve and carried over into the next year may well be considered a form of planned saving.

Notes

1. John A. Wilson, *The Culture of Ancient Egypt* (Chicago: University of Chicago Press, 1951), p. 82.
2. Wilson, *Ancient Egypt,* p. 24; Chester G. Starr, *A History of the Ancient World* (New York: Oxford University Press, 1965), pp. 54, 59; *Encyclopaedia Britannica,* 1929, vol. 8, p. 50; *Encyclopaedia Britannica,* 1968, vol. 8, p. 50.
3. Wilson, *Ancient Egypt,* pp. 80, 87; *Encyclopaedia Britannica,* 1929, vol. 8, p. 53; *Encyclopaedia Britannica,* 1968, vol. 8, p. 53. The term "pharaoh" was not used before the 18th dynasty, c. 1,465 B.C.
4. Wilson, *Ancient Egypt,* pp. 29, 62; Starr, *Ancient World,* p. 59.
5. Adrian Digby, "Boats and Ships," in *A History of Technology,* eds. Charles Singer, E. J. Holmyard, and A. R. Hall (New York: Oxford University Press, 1954), Vol. 1, p. 733; *Encyclopaedia Britannica,* 1929, vol. 8, p. 51; *Encyclopaedia Britannica,* 1968, vol. 8, p. 51.
6. Wilson, *Ancient Egypt,* pp. 82, 101; *Encyclopaedia Britannica,* 1968, pp. 34, 45.
7. Wilson, *Ancient Egypt,* pp. 81, 82; Starr, *Ancient World,* p. 59; *Encyclopaedia Britannica,* 1929, vol. 8, p. 54; *Encyclopaedia Britannica,* 1968, vol. 8, p. 54.
8. Wilson, *Ancient Egypt,* pp. 82, 83; *Encyclopaedia Britannica,* 1929, vol. 8, p. 56, vol. 9, p. 363; vol. 10, p. 418; vol. 12, p. 837; *Encyclopaedia Britannica,* 1968, vol. 8, p. 56.
9. Wilson, *Ancient Egypt,* pp. 37, 38; S. H. Hooke, "Recording and Writing," in *A History of Technology,* eds. Charles Singer, E. J. Holmyard, and A. R. Hall (New York: Oxford University Press, 1954), vol. 1 p. 753.
10. Hooke, "Recording and Writing," pp. 750-57; Starr, *Ancient World,* p. 56.
11. Starr, *Ancient World,* p. 58; *Encyclopaedia Britannica,* 1929, vol. 12, p. 108; vol. 18, p. 792; *Encyclopaedia Britannica,* 1968, vol. 8, p. 48.
12. Herodotus, *The History,* trans. George Rawlinson (New York: E. P. Dutton & Co., 1910), book II, chap. 124, 125; Wilson, *Ancient Egypt,* p. 54;

Starr, *Ancient World,* pp. 58, 59; *Encyclopaedia Britannica,* 1929, vol. 18, p. 899.

13. Herodotus, *The History;* Wilson, *Ancient Egypt,* p. 84; Starr, *Ancient World,* pp. 58, 59; *Encyclopaedia Britannica,* 1929, vol. 8, p. 70; vol. 18, p. 792; *Encyclopaedia Britannica,* 1968, vol. 8, p. 34; vol. 18, p. 895.

14. Wilson, *Ancient Egypt,* p. 79; Starr, *Ancient World,* p. 59.

15. The remains of one such camp that housed about four thousand people can be seen near the second pyramid at Gizeh (*Encyclopaedia Britannica,* 1929, vol. 18, p. 892). We can infer something about living conditions in such a camp from what we are told about them in the Necropolis at West Thebes in connection with a strike of the workers about 1170 B.C. The services provided there included food, water, and laundry service. See Wilson, *Ancient Egypt,* p. 275.

16. Wilson, *Ancient Egypt,* p. 70; Starr, *Ancient World,* pp. 59, 63; S. M. Cole, "Land Transport Without Wheels" in *A History of Technology,* eds. Charles Singer, E. J. Holmyard, and A. R. Hall (New York: Oxford University Press, 1954), vol. 1, p. 714; *Encyclopaedia Britannica,* 1968, vol. 18, p. 895.

17. Wilson, *Ancient Egypt,* pp. 71, 72; O. Neugebauer, "Ancient Mathematics and Astronomy" in *A History of Technology,* eds. Charles Singer, E. J. Holmyard, and A. R. Hall (New York: Oxford University Press, 1954) vol. 1, p. 790; *Encyclopaedia Britannica,* 1929, vol. 8, p. 57; *Encyclopaedia Britannica,* 1968, vol. 8, p. 57.

18. Wilson, *Ancient Egypt,* pp. 30, 61; F. G. Skinner, "Measures and Weights" in *A History of Technology,* eds. Charles Singer, E. J. Holmyard, and A. R. Hall (New York: Oxford University Press, 1954) vol. 1 pp. 774–81; *Webster's New International Dictionary of the English Language,* 2nd ed., unabridged (Springfield, Mass.: G. and G. Merriam Company, 1947), pp. 1521–24, 2898; *Encyclopaedia Britannica,* 1968, vol. 4, p. 620; vol. 23, p. 371; Starr, *Ancient World,* p. 62.

19. Wilson, *Ancient Egypt,* pp. 64, 129–30.

20. *Encyclopaedia Britannica,* 1968, vol. 12, p. 837; vol. 20, p. 198.

21. *Encyclopaedia Britannica,* 1968, vol. 9, p. 363; vol. 10, p. 418.

22. Wilson, *Ancient Egypt,* pp. 55–58; Starr, *Ancient World,* p. 62.

II. The Inca Empire

Legend has it that the Inca Empire was founded by Manco Capac about 1200 or 1000 A.D. At that time, and probably for the next 250 years or more, it was not really an empire; it was just a petty kingdom in the highland region around Cuzco, the capital city. Cuzco has an elevation of some eleven thousand feet.[1]

The Inca culture was a comparatively late comer. Perhaps between 200 B.C. and 200 A.D., there developed not far from the ocean in the region around modern Pisco what is known as the Paracas civilization. There were skilled potters and goldsmiths. But the Paracas people are known especially for their textiles, considered by some connoisseurs to be the best textiles ever produced anywhere. Another great civilization, that of the Tiahuanaco, developed in what is now Bolivia. This civilization may have flourished between 200 and 600 A.D.; some think a good deal later than that. It produced good pottery, tapestry, and human statuary. But it is best known for the great masonry structure built near Lake Titicaca, some 12,500 feet about sea level. There were several other advanced civilizations in the area west of the Andes that preceded the Incas. I shall mention only one of them, that of the Chimu. The Chimu were city dwellers. Their principal city, Chan Chan, had a population estimated at fifty thousand. Its ruins are close to modern Trujillo; they cover about six square miles. It was laid out along straight streets that crossed each other at right angles.[2]

No doubt, the Inca people were in a position to make advantageous combinations of the various techniques they inherited and did so. However, in textiles and pottery, and perhaps in some metal work, they were less skilled than some of their predecessors.[3]

The Empire began with Pachacuti Inca Yupanqui (1438–1471), whose conquests greatly increased the area he ruled. It was much further increased by the conquests of his son, Topa Inca Yupanqui (1471–1493). After Topa's death, not very much more territory was added to the Empire. At its maximum, it extended north to a point on the Ancasmayo River on the border between modern Equador and Colombia and south to the River Maule in modern Chile. Its southern part included a little of modern Argentina. It had an area of about 380,000 square miles and a population estimated at more than sixteen million.[4]

Unlike ancient Egypt, the Inca Empire had almost no trade contacts with the rest of the world around it. It was well provided with metal and other mineral resources and with forest resources; except for what was involved in its conquests, it had no occasion to seek imports.[5]

By ancient custom, the entire population of the Empire was divided into a kind of clan called *ayllus*. An *ayllu* was an extended family; all the members of an *ayllu* considered themselves to be related. Unlike some types of clan, there was no tabu on intermarriage within the *ayllu*. In general, an *ayllu* owned a definite territory. The head of an *ayllu*—he often had the official tile of a *caraca*—had responsibility for settling any disputes that might arise between members, for looking after the welfare of members, and for providing help to any member who needed it.[6]

The Inca state was at once a theocratic monarchy and a socialistic welfare state. There was a large class of nobles and priests whom the rest of the people had to support. The Inca emperor ruled the state autocratically. He was believed to be a lineal descendant of the Sun, the country's principal deity, and he ruled by divine right. Only a few were permitted to enter the emperor's august presence. For many interviews, he was invisible behind a screen. Much of the time he sat on a solid-gold stool called a *tiana*. He drank from a gold or silver cup. Despite all this ceremony, the emperor was greatly concerned for the welfare of the common people. The state's stores of food provided a guarantee that no one should go hungry. But the state regimented the people rigorously.[7]

41

Many of the people were farmers. The government allotted each farm family a plot or plots of arable land, just enough to keep them fed comfortably, assuming an ordinary crop. The allotments were revised each year on the basis of an up-to-date register of the population. There were three categories of arable land: church land, state land, and the land allotted to the farmers. The people in a community were required first to cultivate the church land, next the state land, and after that their own plots. The whole community worked together in cultivating the church land and the state land. When their obligations on the church land and the state land had been discharged, each family cultivated its own plot or plots. Both in the community operations and on their own plots, the men and women worked together, singing as they worked. The principal crops were white potatoes, maize, and sweet potatoes. Various other crops were raised, too, among them peanuts, avocados, tomatoes, manioc, beans, and cotton. Presumably, custom was the chief determinant of what was raised.[8]

There were in the Empire quite a number of hundred thousand llamas, a somewhat smaller number of alpacas, and a still smaller number of vicuñas. There was a great deal of grazing land. There was a three-way division of the livestock and the grazing land. There were: (1) livestock and grazing land that belonged to the church; (2) livestock and grazing land that belonged to the state; and (3) livestock and grazing land allotted to individuals, some of it to nobles, the rest of it to commoners. The herdsmen who were commoners had responsibility first for taking care of the church livestock on the church land and next for taking care of the state livestock on the state land; after that, they looked after the llamas and alpacas allotted to them on the grazing land allotted to them. The wool from the church livestock was church property; the wool from the state livestock was state property. A good deal of the wool from the other livestock went to the state as a tax. The wives of the herdsmen had the rest; from it, they made yarn, then cloth, and then clothing. There were women attached to the temples who combed and spun the church wool into yarn and made the yarn into cloth and tapestries. There were state employees who processed some of the state wool; but most of it was doled out to state employees and others for their womenfolk to make into clothing and cloth for household use.

The vicuñas were never domesticated; they just ran wild. From time to time, a large-scale hunt was organized; in such a hunt, perhaps more than a thousand men might be employed. The vicuñas were herded into a corral where they were sheared and then released. The fine vicuña wool was reserved for the use of the Inca and other nobles.[9]

In the case of Egypt, in spite of the great difference between the culture of ancient Egypt and the culture of a twentieth-century industrialized country, we divided the population of ancient Egypt into (a) the labor force and (b) all other persons, just as we divide our population today. We think this led to no misinterpretation. And despite the great cultural disparity between the Incas and the United States today, we think a similar division of the Empire's population will lead to no misinterpretation, so we shall make it. Because the Inca economy, like that of ancient Egypt, was predominatly agricultural, the farm families and the herdsmen were numerically a very large part of the Inca labor force. The skilled craftsmen were a relatively small, but a very important group of workers. There were masons, carpenters, gold and silversmiths, coppersmiths, and various others, among them the men who kept the up-to-date register of the population. These men were called *quipucamayocs*. All of the craftsmen were government employees, and as such, together with their families, were provided with housing, food, wool, and other amenities.[10]

Among other members of the labor force, there were three categories of persons, each of which represneteed a distinctively Inca type of occupaton. (1) There were *yanacuna,* sons of commoners who had been separated from their *ayllus* when young and given the status of a special kind of servant. A *yanacuna* might be made a servant of the Inca or of one of the nobles. If he were assigned to a noble who had an allotment

43

of livestock he might be expected to serve as a herdsman. If he were assigned to the Inca, he might be made a page, or he might be given supervisory or other work that might enable him to rise to a position of some importance. The young men who became *yanacuna* had, in general, been selected because of their intelligence, ability, or promise.[11]

(2) A young girl, when she was about ten years old, was carefully inspected by a government inspector. Girls who were physically perfect and particularly beautiful were selected to attend a kind of finishing school. There they spent some four years studying domestic science, religion, weaving, and how to make *chicha,* the Inca corn beer. When they had completed their education, a few of them might be selected for human sacrifice on some great state occasion. To be so selected was a great and apparently a much-coveted honor that assured after-life happiness. Most of them, however, became *nustas* or *acllacuna* or "chosen women." Many *acllacuna* were chosen by noblemen as secondary wives or as concubines. A particularly fortunate one might be chosen by the Inca himself. Occasionally, there might be an *acllacuna* whom no nobleman chose as a secondary wife or a concubine. Such an one became a *mamacuna,* a mother superior in the finishing school.[12]

(3) Some girls, when they had completed their finishing-school education, were consecrated to service to the Sun and became "Virgins of the Sun." They were sworn to permanent chastity. They served in a convent attached to a temple dedicated to the Sun. Some of them served in the convent attached to Coricancha, the great Temple of the Sun in Cuzco, a convent presided over by a priestess of noble birth who was considered to be the wife of the Sun. But many "Virgins of the Sun" served in convents attached to temples dedicated to the Sun in other Inca cities. The duties of "Virgins of the Sun" included weaving fine textiles that were used in religious ceremonies and preparing the *chicha* that was used in religious festivals.[13]

In addition to those already discussed, there were a number of other members of the labor force. Perhaps the largest group consisted of the priests and the underlings attached to

44

the various temples. There were also a good many government officials, army officers as well as civil officials. The only full-time soldiers in addition to the army officers were apparently the members of the Inca's bodyguard. To this list of persons who were members of the labor force we should add at least one other group. There were women who had lost their connections with their *ayllus* and become prostitutes.[14]

A variety of foods was available to the commoners as well as to the nobles, much of it in the form of a soup or a stew. A porridge was made from a kind of pigweed or from oca roots. Some maize was dried and ground into corn meal, but often maize was served as corn on the cob. Sweet potatoes and, in the highlands, white potatoes were important foods. Llama meat was cut into thin strips and dried. In this form—it was called *charqui*—it kept well. Men liked to chew coca leaves mixed with lime; but this drug was apparently available to commoners only on special occasions. Everyone drank *chicha,* an intoxicating beverage made mostly from maize, sometimes from pigweed or oca. There were a good many holidays on which people got very drunk. Among the foods a good many people enjoyed were peanuts, beans, avocados, tomatoes, and squash.[15]

Despite its extensive division of labor, the Inca Empire was definitely a nonmoney economy. There were indeed holidays which were, among other things, market days, three of them each month. People brought things to these fairs that they hoped to swap. But there was not only no medium of exchange, there was also no standard of value for such exchange transactions. And, of course, there were no taxes payable in money or a substitute for it, only a tax paid in personal services.[16]

This tax, called the *mita,* was imposed on all able-bodied men except the nobles, the priests, craftsmen and other government employees, and the *yanacuna.* Each taxpayer was required to do a certain amount of work for the government each year. The work took various forms. For farmers some of it was work in cultivating church and state farm land, and for herdsmen it was taking care of church and state livestock. *Mita* service also included work on public construction and other government projects, work on water conduits and irrigation canals, work in the mines and on roads and bridges, and military service. One type of *mita* service to which we shall presently give special attention was performed by the young men who provided the Empire with its postal sevice.[17]

The Empire was divided into four sectors, or *suyus*, by two major highways that intersected at Cuzco. One of these highways ran generally north through Quito to the Ancasmayo River and south to the River Maule. The other ran roughly east and west. Just how the line was drawn between the two western *suyus* is not clear, probably from Cuzco to Nazca. Nor is it clear how the line between the two eastern *suyus* was drawn, perhaps from Cuzco through Pisac to Paucartambo. The Inca people thought of the four *suyus* as the four quarters of the world. Each *suyu* was governed by a viceroy called an *apo*, who reported directly to the Inca. Each of them was probably a close relative of the Inca.[18]

There were two standards of improper and punishable conduct, one for the nobles, the other for commoners. For the latter, not only treason and disobedience of the Inca but also stealing from church or government fields or warehouses, destroying a bridge, or breaking into a *nusta* convent as well as murder were crimes punishable by death. Judgment in any such case was passed only by the Inca or an *apo*. Guilt was sometimes determined by divination or by an ordeal such as torture. The sentence might be executed by bashing in the head of the culprit with a club, throwing him off a high cliff, or stoning him. Minor offenses such as laziness, improvidence, dishonesty, drunkenness when one should be working, or inflicting a minor injury on another person were judged by less important officials. Punishment might take the form of exile to the mines, flogging, torture, or simply a public rebuke.

All crimes committed by nobles were judged by the Inca himself. Apparently there were very few of them. A nobleman was a kind of government official. Capital crimes included treason and adultery between a nobleman and a noble woman. The penalty for the latter type of crime was death for both parties. Sometimes the Inca reprimanded a noble for something he had done. Even a public reprimand was, in effect, a very severe punishment.[19]

The remains of the great fortress, Sacsahuaman, are only a short distance north and east of Cuzco. Apparently it was built not to protect the capital city, but to provide a refuge for its population in the event of a serious enemy attack. Not much remains of its buildings and towers. There were three great walls; one of them had a maximum height of some sixty feet. Each wall was quite long; one of them eighteen hundred feet. There were reservoirs to provide water in case the fortress was besieged.

Just how this fortress was built we can only surmise. Its construction was certainly a very great engineering feat, comparable to that of the construction of the Great Pyramid at Gizeh, although probably a somewhat smaller number of man-hours was employed on it. Like the Egyptian pyramids, it was built without the aid of wheeled vehicles, pulleys, or cranes, and without iron tools. It was made of huge blocks of stone rectangular parallelepipeds, one of them said to be seventeen feet high, ten feet wide, and nine feet thick, and to have weighed something over a hundred tons. It and the other huge blocks were carefully trimmed and precisely fitted into place. Tradition has it that thirty thousand men were employed on this Herculean undertaking.[20]

Sacsahuaman was by no means the only extremely impressive Inca construction work the remains of which can still be seen. There were two great fortresses on the Urubamba River within twenty-five miles of Cuzco. This river is a tributary of the Ucayali which in turn is a tributary of the Amazon. The remains of the fortress at Pisac do not tell us too much about what it was like. Downstream at Ollantaytambo, there rises from the east bank of the river a great set of agricultural terraces carved into the rocky face of the hillside. Above them on the acropolis are the remains of the fortress and also six great stone blocks that were to have formed the base of an impressive Sun Temple. The work on this fortress was still in process when the Spaniards took over in 1536.

At Ollantaytambo there was a major *nusta* convent, and to the right of the base of the great flight of agricultural terraces there was a bathing pool that was reserved for the use of the *nustas*.

On the western bank of the river can be seen the remains of a stone quarry that tell us something about the Inca quarrying operations. Like other people with not much in the way of mechanical equpment, to split a great rock they took advantage of any natural faults, bored a hole in it, inserted a wooden wedge in the hole, and then soaked the wedge with water, relying on its swelling to crack the rock.[21]

Facing the principal square at one corner of the intersection of the two major highways in the center of Cuzco stood Coricancha, the magnificent Temple of the Sun. Unfortunately, not much of it remains today, only the great stone masonry structure that was its base. On this has been built the Church of Santo Domingo. For our ideas about what the Temple was like we are forced to rely on reports written by some of the Spanish conquistadores who saw it when it was intact. It seems to have been a rectangular structure, the outside walls of which were sheathed with heavy sheets of gold. The principal room, called the Hall of the Sun, was perhaps more than ninety feet long and forty-five feet wide. It was the repository of various sacred objects, among them solid-gold idols of the major deities, the bodies of recent Incas, and possibly solid-gold, life-size statues of them. There was also, if we can believe the reports written about Coricancha, an imitation garden in which there were life-size golden replicas of growing maize plants bearing realistic-looking ears; and there were life-size statues of llamas cast in gold that grazed on the golden corn stalks.

In each of the other major cities, there was an impressive Temple of the Sun, although none of them approached Coricancha in Cuzco in splendor. There were also a number of palaces. In Cuzco, there were several. When an Inca died, it was thought that his spirit continued to dwell in his palace; hence, his successor built himself a new palace.[22]

Machu Picchu was a little city built on a mountain side some fourteen hundred feet above a point on the Urubamba River some miles north of Ollantaytambo to which a train from Cuzco now runs once a day. Because Machu Picchu was pretty inaccessible, it was never discovered by the conquistadores. It was not discovered by white men until 1911. It can only be reached by a road that zigzags up the mountain side and on which there are fourteen sharp elbow turns. The city is practically intact except that the roofs of the buildings which were made of thatch are gone and except that articles made of gold and other easily portable valuables have been removed. The city was probably able to accommodate about five hundred people. Some of them were *nustas;* doubtless, some of them were high officials who hid out there. The more important buildings are masonry structures made of large stone blocks, rectangular parallelepipeds except for their faces that protrude slightly from the lines of the building; the faces are smooth, rough stone. One of the buildings was a Temple of the Sun, one a palace, and one a *nusta* convent. There is still a fountain that is fed by water that comes down from higher up the mountain. Included in the city are a series of masonry agricultural terraces. The road up the mountain entered the city over a narrow passage with a cliff on one side and a gorge on the other. There was a wooden gate that could close off the entryway; but, in any case, the entryway was easily defensible.[23]

The Inca highway system was built primarily for the military forces to travel and to facilitate the transportation of military supplies. There were two main north-south highways, the one through the highlands, whose terminals we have just noted—it was about 3,250 miles long—and one that ran for about 2,500 miles along the coast from Tumbez in what is now northern Peru through Ariquipa and possibly into what is modern Chile. The highland road much of the way was only three feet wide. There were sections of it that zigzagged up hills, some even that were essentially stairways. There were cuts through solid rock and more than one tunnel. There were causeways over marshy places—one of them near Cuzco that was eight miles long and twenty-four feet wide—and there were masonry bridges. There were numerous culverts to provide adequate drainage.

Most of the coastal road was wider, twelve to fifteen feet. There were stretches that were paved, especially those that went through cities. On some stretches, there were stone walls along one side or along both sides. Along some stretches, there were shade trees. There were also parts of this road that ran through desert territory, parts which consisted merely of a line of posts on either side that marked the trail. The highway system included, in addition to the two great north-south roads and the east-west road through Cuzco, a considerable number of other roads that ran roughly east and west.

In Cuzco and other cities there were paved streets. Some of them had a stone wall along one side, some a stone wall on either side. Several of the street walls in Cuzco, and doubtless in other places, were carefully built masonry structures that consisted of nicely trimmed and nicely placed rectangular parallelepedic stone blocks. Each block represented somewhat more than a cubic foot of stone, and like the blocks in the walls of the principal buildings at Machu Picchu, the face of each block was left roughhewn and protruded slightly from the line of the wall. There were street walls in Cuzco a good deal more than ten feet tall.[24]

The Incas built various types of bridges. Where a stream ws small enough to be spanned by a single large stone, the bridge was a masonry structure. Logs were often used for a longer span. There were places at which pontoon bridges were built; the floats were sometimes rafts, sometimes small boats. A number of deep chasms were crossed by suspension bridges. Each such bridge consisted primarily of five cables. The cables were made of vines braided together or long thin twigs twisted together. Some cables were as much as sixteen inches in diameter. At each end of the bridge each cable was firmly anchored to a beam imbedded in a masonry pier. Three of the cables, together with sticks and matting laid across them, constituted the floor of the bridge; the other two served as railings. Each such bridge was kept in good repair at all times; the upkeep was a *mita* obligation of people living in the vicinity. Since there were no stays a bridge swayed in the wind or when a man or a llama was using it. The cables of the bridge across the Apurimac River, made famous by Thornton Wilder's story about it, were some three hundred feet long.[25]

In addition to its fortresses and other public buildings, public works in the Inca Empire took a form that must have substantially increased its agricultural production. Many hillsides and even mountain sides were effectively terraced to add to the amount of arable land. There is a spectacular series of agricultural terraces on the hillside to the east of Pisac. This kind of land was irrigated by water that started at the top and dribbled down from terrace to terrace. And the terracing substantially retarded soil erosion.[26]

The Empire had a very ingenious and extensive system of canals, water conduits, and reservoirs. The water channels were nicely engineered to provide suitable gradients. At various places the water was carried across valleys on aqueducts. Most of this water-supply system, like the Empire's fortresses, bridges, and other structures, was doubtless planned by Inca engineers and built by Inca workmen. But part of it was inherited. At Ascope, some miles north of modern Trujillo, there is found one of the great engineering accomplishments of ancient Peru, an aqueduct nearly a mile long that carried water over a ravine some fifty feet deep. And past a point not far from it, there runs a seventy-five-mile canal that is still in use. Both the aqueduct and the canal were probably built before 600 A.D.[27]

The main purpose of the Inca water-supply system was certainly providing irrigation water. But it provided some cities with a supply that served personal requirements. In Cuxco the streams running through the city were channeled in canals. And the canalized streams provided some buildings and some baths with running water.[28]

Along each Inca highway, and even on lesser roads, there were stations called *tambos*. A *tambo* was a kind of rest house at which a travelling official could get food or spend the night. Weapons and military supplies as well as food were stored at each *tambo*. On the main highways, the distance between one *tambo* and the next was what was considered to be a day's journey for a high travelling official, twelve to eighteen miles, depending on the terrain. Some *tambos* were luxuriously equipped, ready to entertain the Inca himself, if his travels took him that way. A local offical was responsible for the operation of each *tambo*.[29]

The Empire had an excellent postal service. Young men in good health were trained as distance runners, and each, at least as a part of his *mita* service, was required to be a *chasqui* for a period of fifteen days. There were on almost every road stations at which the *chasquis* or runners were kept on duty, apparently two of them on each side of the road. Since the service operated around the clock, there must have been a shift arrangement. The *chasquis* carried messages, usually in the form of a record, to be considered shortly, called a *quipu;* they also carried small parcels. The minute a *chasqui* on the run arrived at a station, he delivered the message he was carrying and the parcel, if any, to one of the *chasquis* on duty there. This man then ran with the message and the parcel, if any, at top speed to the next station and passed it (or them) on to a *chasqui* on duty there to be carried farther forward. With this relay system, a message could travel from Quito to Cuzco, a distance of 1,250 miles, in five days. This meant an average speed of between ten and eleven miles an hour. Since a number of the *chasquis* were running at altitudes of over ten thousand feet, they may have had coca leaves mixed with lime to chew. The parcels post service seems to have brought fresh fish from the coast to the Inca in Cuzco in two days.[30]

For simple yes-and-no messages, the Empire had a somewhat faster method of transmitting them. Smoke signals were used.[31]

The only beast of burden the Empire had was the llama.

Llamas seldom served as mounts; they did not pull plows; the cows were not milked. A llama would carry a load of not much more than a hundred pounds on his back; he balked if overloaded. Llamas were sure-footed and they were not bothered by the altitudes of the upper north-south highway. For freight transportation, they were driven in trains of several hundred animals, one driver for about a hundred of them. A train did not go very fast, nine to twelve miles a day.[32]

The Inca and other nobles and high government officials travelled around the Empire in palanquins. Four bearers carried one of these carriages on two long poles, one on either side. On some palanquins there were seats for two people. The finer ones had canopies for shade. The one in which the Inca travelled had mantles that enclosed him from public view when he wished to be so enclosed. On his travels he seems often to have made various stops by the wayside. At some of these, he gave local officials an opportunity to consult him about decisions they were having to make. At others, he gave his subjects an audience and listened to whatever they wished to tell him about their problems. His palanquin was decorated with gold and embroidery and precious stones. It was considered a great honor to be a bearer of the Inca's palanquin. The bearers served in relays. When he travelled for any considerable distance, quite a number of bearers went with him, perhaps enough so that no one had more than one spell of duty.[33]

There were apparently a number of routes travelled by Inca officials that included water crossings too long to be bridged. At each such place, local officals maintained a ferry service. Most ferries were probably boats made of tortora reeds; some may have been balsa log rafts. Each ferry must have been big enough to carry the palanquin and the people who travelled with the official, perhaps more than a dozen people.[34]

A *quipu* consisted of a heavy horizontal string and a number of lighter strings suspended from it which were of different colors and twists and in which various knots were tied. Significance attached to the colors and twists and to the type and position of each knot. In some *quipus,* there were more than a hundred pendant strings. It is certain that some pendant strings recorded a quantity of something, one for the something and perhaps three or four for the quantity. We know that a place-value number notation was used; a zero digit seems to have been represented by the absence of a knot where it was otherwise to be expected. Most of the numbers symbolized were one-, two-, three-, and four-place numbers; only one instance of a five-place number is known. Relatively few of the *quipus* that have survived are known to be complete; it is difficult to be sure there are no missing strings. One *quipu* may, of course, have recorded the quantities of two or more somethings; but it seems clear that *quipus* were used to record historical and other nonquantitative facts, such as the life and activities of the Inca. *Quipus* were not calculating devices. No surviving *quipu* seems to have been fully and noncontroversially deciphered. There were Spanish priests who thought *quipus* were "books of the devil"; many of them were sanctimoniously destroyed.[35]

Inca engineers had what it seems clear was a calculating device, a kind of abacus. What we know about it comes from a picture drawn by a conquistador. The picture is mainly designed to show what a *quipu* looks like, but in the lower left-hand corner a face-view of this calculating device is shown. On it there are twenty small squares arranged in four columns and five rows. In each square in the left-hand column, there are three dots in a vertical line at the left and two in a vertical line at the right. In each square in the next column, there are two dots in a vertical line at the left and a single dot at the right. In each square in the third column, two dots in a vertical line are centered; and in the fourth and right-hand column, there is a single dot at the center. It is assumed that the dots represent buttons or other play pieces that could be moved from the positions described to other positions.[36]

Inca engineers did not make mechanical drawings in planning buildings, terraces, and city layouts. But they had a fairly good substitute; they made scale models in clay. Some of these models have survived.[37]

The system of weights and measures used in the Inca Empire seems to have been well standardized. Two measures of distance were the fathom, about 64 inches (162 cm.) and the *topo,* about 4 1/2 miles (7.25 km.). There were also smaller distance measures based on parts of the human body. There was an area measure called a *topo,* too; this was equal to something over an acre, 45,000 square feet (41.8 acres). There was a measure for grain equal to about five-sixths of a bushel (29 litres). Weight was measured with a balance-beam type of scale.[38]

The sons of high officials of a newly conquered territory who wanted to become loyal Inca citizens were sent to a school or college that was established to offer them suitable training. There was a four-year course of study they were expected to pursue. The first year was devoted to *quechua,* the Inca language, the second to Inca religion, the third to the *quipu,* the fourth to the Empire's history. Young Inca nobles who planned to become administrators took some of the courses this college offered.[39]

We shall deal only very briefly with a subject about which much as been written, Inca arts and crafts. Various types of weaving were experimented with; most woven goods were produced to be used as clothing. But in the temples Virgins of the Sun produced particularly fine tapestries. Inca potters—they were men—simply took over the techniques they had inherited from their Guañape predecessors. They did not have a wheel. They were extremely skilled workmen. Some of the gold and silver ornaments that have survived, particularly those made in the northern part of the Empire, were very dainty and exquisite castings.[40]

The Empire's military establishment was vastly superior to that of any enemy it encountered before the coming of the Spaniards. It is true the army's equipment was about as primitive as that of the peoples it fought with. The soldiers had slings, each about six feet long with a cradle for the stone in the middle. They also had bolas; a bola was a projectile that consisted of a number of stones on the ends of strings fastened together at the end of a cord or thong so that the bola could be whirled and thrown with considerable force. For close combat the principal weapon was a heavy club with a rough stone or a star-shaped hunk of bronze at the end. There were also spears and heavy wooden swords. Some of the spears had fire-hardened tips; some had copper or bronze tips.

The soldiers wore long, heavy, quilted cotton shirts and helmets made of wood or plaited cane. Some carried small round or rectangular shields. To protect a number of men engaged in a siege operation, the army had a large sheet of strong cloth that served as a testudo.[41]

The Empire went to war only after due deliberation. Strenuous efforts were made to gain the objective without fighting, by negotiation. If this did not succeed, there was a religious ceremony in which priests offered prayers for supernatural aid and in which half-starved black llamas were sacrificed. The heart of a sacrificed llama was carefully studied; if some of the flesh near the heart had been absorbed, this was a favorable omen. Before fighting began, drums were beaten and trumpets were blown. The initial period in which stones were slung and bolas were thrown was quite short. The battle soon became one of hand-to-hand combat.[42]

The superiority of the Inca army was in part one of sheer numbers and of skillful management by clever generals. It was not a standing army, only a large number of commoners drafted for the occasion operating under rigid discipline. But there was another very important factor in the superiority of the Inca army: it was provisioned by a particularly efficient commissariat. And, of course, with its system of roads and *tambos* and its postal service, the Empire was prepared to deal promptly and effectively with any uprising that might occur.[43]

When a new territory was added to the Empire, a census was taken not only of its population but also of its resources, livestock, arable and grazing land, water supply, etc. The findings were recorded both on *quipus* and on clay relief models. Steps were taken to impose the Inca culture on the people, land and livestock allotments, the various forms of *mita* service, worship of the Sun, learning to speak *quechua*, Inca costumes, etc. None the less, care was taken to avoid making more changes in people's ways than was necessary and to permit them to keep many of their established customs. For whatever seemed needed in the way of new buildings, roads, bridges, etc., a construction program was undertaken. The country's principal idols as well as the sons of nobles were taken to Cuzco as hostages. In some cases, the conquest resulted in making the people more civilized, in the adoption of improved agricultural techniques, and in a higher level of living for the conquered people.[44]

The treatment of a conquered people depended very largely on their willingness to adopt Inca ways. If they were recalcitrant, particularly if they were bellicose, most of them were deported and required to live in an area assigned to them. Settlers were brought in to replace them. There were in the Empire people who were loyal citizens and who were willing to participate in the imperial resettlement program and to inculcate Inca culture. These people, called *mitimaes,* were granted special privileges for their participation in the program.[45]

On the whole, the Empire seems to have been very successful in getting people in conquered territories to adopt Inca ways. *Quechua* quite rapidly became the language spoken everywhere.[46]

The Inca people considered that by nature they were superior to other human beings. They seem to have chosen to believe that none of the civilizations that had preceded theirs had much merit. In fact, they were apparently concerned to destroy records of the achievements of their predecessors. The history that was taught in their college probably assumed that civilization began with the Empire.[47]

Notes

1. J. Alden Mason, *The Ancient Civilizations of Peru* (Harmondsworth, Middlesex, England: Penguin Books Ltd., 1957), pp. 111–12; Victor W. Von Hagen, *Realm of the Incas* (New York: New American Library, 1957), p. 34; William H. Prescott, *The World of the Incas* (Geneva: Editions Minerva, 1970), pp. 8–11; *Encyclopaedia Britannica*, 1968, vol. 1, p. 890; vol. 6, p. 932.

2. Mason, *Peru,* 65–68, 91–94, 100–02; Von Hagen, *Realm of the Incas,* pp. 23–24, 27–31, 148, 156; Prescott, *The World of Incas,* pp. 9–10; *Encylopaedia Britannica,* 1968, vol. 1, pp. 889; vol. 5, p. 264.
3. *Encyclopaedia Britannica,* 1968, vol. 1, p. 891.
4. Mason, *Peru,* pp. 120–28, 131, 138; Von Hagen, *Realm of the Incas,* pp. 117, 132, 158; *Encyclopaedia Britannica,* 1968, vol. 1, pp. 725, 890; vol. 6, p. 932; vol. 20, p. 997.
5. *Encyclopaedia Britannica,* 1929, vol. 1, pp. 905–06; vol. 9, p. 502, vol. 17, p. 868; vol. 21, p. 70; *Encyclopaedia Britannica,* 1968, vol. 17, p. 711.
6. Mason, *Peru,* pp. 174–77; Von Hagen, *Realm of the Incas,* p. 46; *Encyclopaedia Britannica,* 1968, vol. 20, p. 997.
7. Mason, *Peru,* pp. 185–91; Von Hagen, *Realm of the Incas,* pp. 113–16, 120, 121, 124; Prescott, *The World of Incas,* pp. 15–16, 18–19, 24, 53–54, 72, 90, 98–99, 124; *Encyclopaedia Britannica,* 1968, vol. 1, pp. 890, 891; vol. 20, p. 997.
8. Mason, *Peru,* pp. 141, 179–82; Von Hagen, *Realm of the Incas,* pp. 58–60, 64–65; Prescott, *The World of Incas,* pp. 40, 42, 49–50, 103, 104; *Encyclopaedia Britannica,* 1968, vol. 1, p. 890.
9. Mason, *Peru,* pp. 140, 144, 183, 245; Von Hagen, *Realm of the Incas,* p. 78; Prescott, *The World of Incas,* pp. 43, 106, 107.
10. Mason, *Peru,* p. 184; Von Hagen, *Realm of the Incas,* pp. 88, 158; *Encyclopaedia Britannica,* 1968, vol. 1, p. 891.
11. Mason, *Peru,* p. 184; *Encyclopaedia Britannica,* 1968, vol. 1, p. 891.
12. Mason, *Peru,* p. 185; Von Hagen, *Realm of the Incas,* pp. 55–56, 123, 125, 128, 158–59; Prescott, *The World of Incas,* p. 84; *Encyclopedia Britannica,* 1968, vol. 1, p. 891.
13. Mason, *Peru,* p. 185; Von Hagen, *Realm of the Incas,* pp. 133, 143, 209; Prescott, *The World of Incas,* pp. 84, 86, 89, 90; *Encyclopaedia Britannica,* 1968, vol. 1, p. 891.
14. Mason, *Peru,* pp. 180, 184-85, 193; Von Hagen, *Realm of the Incas,* pp. 88, 151; Prescott, *The World of Incas,* pp. 80, 82, 94, 95, 97.
15. Mason, *Peru,* pp. 141, 145-47; Von Hagen, *Realm of the Incas,* pp. 52–53, 77; Prescott, *The World of Incas,* pp. 103, 107; *Encyclopaedia Britannica,* 1968, vol. 1, p. 890.
16. Mason, *Peru,* pp. 172, 193; Von Hagen, *Realm of the Incas,* pp. 90-91; Prescott, *The World of Incas,* pp. 38, 102, 111.
17. Mason, *Peru,* 167, 171, 180, 183, 192, 193; Von Hagen, *Realm of the Incas,* 64, 71–73, 125; *Encyclopaedia Britannica,* 1968, vol. 1, p. 891; vol. 20, p. 997.
18. Von Hagen, *Realm of the Incas,* pp. 154 ff; Prescot, *The World of Incas,* pp. 35, 37; *Encyclopaedia Britannica,* 1968, vol. 20, p. 997.
19. Mason, *Peru,* pp. 203–5; Von Hagen, *Realm of the Incas,* pp. 99–101; Prescott, *The World of Incas,* pp. 38–39, 46, 53.
20. Mason, *Peru,* 163–64, 180, 197, plates 15 A and B; Von Hagen, *Realm of the Incas,* pp. 145–49, 154; Prescott, *The World of Incas,* pp. 12, 15; *Encyclopaedia Britannica,* 1968, vol. 1, p. 891; vol. 6, p. 932.
21. Mason, *Peru,* pp. 142, 163, plate 17; Von Hagen, *Realm of the Incas,* pp. 66, 137–38, 147, 154.
22. Mason, *Peru,* pp. 136, 162, 208, 211–12, plate 13; Von Hagen, *Realm*

of the Incas, pp. 128–30, 133, 151; Prescott, *The World of Incas,* pp. 12, 79, 80, 83.

23. Mason, *Peru,* p. 163; Von Hagen, *Realm of the Incas,* pp. 14–15, 50, 139–40.

24. Mason, *Peru,* pp. 165–55, plate 12; Von Hagen, *Realm of the Incas,* pp. 131, 161–65; Prescott, *The World of Incas,* p. 66; *Encyclopaedia Britannica,* 1968, vol. 1, p. 891. Von Hagen, who made an extensive study of the Inca road system, insists that "the standard width of the Inca coastal road was twenty-four feet" and that it was this wide for a thousand miles. He must have included the trees that grew along the road and the walls built along it.

25. Mason, *Peru,* p. 167; Von Hagen, *Realm of the Incas,* pp. 165, 167-72; Prescott, *The World of Incas,* 57, 59; *Encyclopaedia Britannica,* 1968, vol. 1, p. 891.

26. Mason, *Peru,* pp. 141–42, 168, 181; Von Hagen, *Realm of the Incas,* pp. 66–67, plate 3; Prescott, *The World of Incas,* pp. 7, 100; *Encyclopaedia Britannica,* 1968, vol. 1, p. 891; vol, 20, p. 997.

27. Mason, *Peru,* pp. 142, 167–68, 181; Von Hagen, *Realm of the Incas,* pp. 66-67; Prescott, *The World of Incas,* pp. 7, 99–100; *Encyclopaedia Britannica,* 1968, vol. 1, p. 891.

28. Mason, *Peru,* p. 168.

29. Mason, *Peru,* pp. 166-67; Von Hagen, *Realm of the Incas,* pp. 133, 173–76; Prescott, *The World of the Incas,* pp. 20, 60; *Encyclopaedia Britannica,* 1968, vol. 20, p. 997.

30. Mason, *Peru,* p. 171; Von Hagen, *Realm of the Incas,* pp. 71, 108, 157, 181–94, 206; Prescott, *The World of Incas,* pp. 60, 63; *Encyclopaedia Britannica,* 1968, vol. 1, p. 891; vol. 20, p. 997. According to Von Hagen, the ancient Romans had a system for carrying messages that employed couriers who were mounted on horseback and who operated in relays. He says, "One hundred miles a day was considered very good time" for a message to make under this system. The Inca postal service carried a message 250 miles in a day.

31. Mason, *Peru,* p. 171.

32. Mason, *Peru,* pp. 144–45, 169; Von Hagen, *Realm of the Incas,* pp. 78, 177; Prescott, *The World of Incas,* p. 105.

33. Mason, *Peru,* pp. 169-70, 188, 192; Von Hagen, *Realm of the Incas,* pp. 115, 121–22, 178; Prescott, *The World of Incas,* pp. 20, 63.

34. Mason, *Peru,* pp. 167, 171–72; Von Hagen, *Realm of the Incas,* p. 179.

35. Mason, *Peru,* pp. 230–34; Von Hagen, *Realm of the Incas,* pp. 157, 185–87; Prescott, *The World of Incas,* pp. 60, 94–96; *Encyclopaedia Britannica,* 1968, vol. 1, p. 891; vol. 18, p. 970; vol. 20, p. 997.

36. Mason, *Peru,* pp. 233-34; Von Hagen, *Realm of the Incas,* p. 147.

37. Mason, *Peru,* p. 200; Von Hagen, *Realm of the Incas,* p. 147.

38. Mason, *Peru,* pp. 167, 234; Von Hagen, *Realm of the Incas,* pp. 49, 162; Prescott, *The World of Incas,* p. 111.

39. Mason, *Peru,* p. 191; Prescott, *The World of Incas,* pp. 93–94.

40. Mason, *Peru,* pp. 253, 267, 269–70; Von Hagen, *Realm of the Incas,* pp. 82–83, 85–86, 151, 153.

41. Mason, *Peru,* pp. 195–96; Von Hagen, *Realm of the Incas,* pp. 106, 196–97, 199; Prescott, *The World of Incas,* p. 64.

42. Mason, *Peru,* pp. 195–99; Von Hagen, *Realm of the Incas,* pp. 196, 199.

43. Mason, *Peru*, pp. 196–97; Von Hagen, *Realm of the Incas*, p. 199.
44. Mason, *Peru*, pp. 201–3; Von Hagen, *Realm of the Incas*, pp. 201–3 *Encyclopaedia Britannica*, 1968, vol. 1, p. 891; Prescott, *The World of Incas*, pp. 67–68, 71, 114.
45. Mason, *Peru*, pp. 201–2; Von Hagen, *Realm of the Incas*, pp. 156, 160, 202; Prescott, *The World of Incas*, pp. 72, 102; *Encyclopaedia Britannica*, 1968, vol. 1, p. 891; vol. 20, p. 997.
46. Mason, *Peru*, pp. 201–2; Von Hagen, *Realm of the Incas*, pp. 45, 202–3; Prescott, *The World of Incas*, p. 72; *Encyclopaedia Britannica*, 1968, vol. 1, p. 725.
47. Mason, *Peru*, p. 198; Von Hagen, *Realm of the Incas*, pp. 116, 118, 188.

Resemblances and Differences

The Inca Empire was much larger than Egypt in the days of the Old Kingdom, and the problems of governing it were, therefore, significantly greater. The Empire's population by 1470 A.D. was probably more than ten times that of Egypt. Nominally the areas of the two countries were about the same. But no part of Egypt where people lived was more than a short distance from the Nile. In the Inca Empire, on the other hand, *chasquis* travelled north and south between Quito and the River Maule, a distance of some three thousand miles, and east and west between the Pacific Ocean and various inland places, among them Cuzco, eleven thousand above seal level and about 160 miles inland.

Each country had a totalitarian government. Each was a planned economy. In an economy such as ours we rely to a large extent on economic institutions, the price system, trade, markets, the profit system, and freedom of enterprise, to determine (1) what is to be produced; (2) who is to do what; and (3) who is to get what. Let us consider how these three basic central management functions were performed in each of these two totalitarian, planned economies.

(1) It is true that in neither of them was the composition of the gross national product planned in every detail. In both of them much of it was determined by the rule that each man or woman should continue doing what he or she knew how to do and had been doing. Thus, the fellahin in Egypt continued to cultivate the land they had inherited and to look after their livestock. Similarly, the farm people in the Inca Empire cultivated the plots of land allotted to them and the church and state land in their area, and the herdsmen tended the llamas and alpacas allotted to them and the church and state livestock for which they were responsible. In Egypt, improvements in the water-control and irrigation system may in some years have resulted in new arable land. Allotting this land involved a kind of economic planning. And, of course, the annual allotments of land and livestock by the Inca government were

planned. Otherwise, the detailed planning of production in both countries was the planning involved in particular government undertakings. In the case of Egypt these were: (a) Nile water control and irrigation system projects; (b) mining expeditions into Sinai and elsewhere; (c) trading expeditions, including bringing in lumber from Byblos and olive oil, wine, and other things from Syria and elsewhere; and (d) pyramid and other construction projects. In the case of the Inca Empire they were: (a) the construction of public buildings and fortresses and roads, streets, and bridges; (b) the terracing of hillsides; and (c) work on its water-conduit system.

(2) To a large extent, too, who was to do what in each economy was determined by the rule that each person was to continue doing the things expected of him or her in the occupation he or she had inherited. In the case of Egypt, this was clearly true of the fellahin and probably true of some of the things done by some priests and some government officials and other government employees. It was true of the Inca Empire's farm people and herdsmen; and, in the Empire, too, of some of the things done by some priests and by some government officials and other government employees. In Egypt, there were clearly specific job assignments for the men engaged in a mining or a trading expedition, also for men working on a water-control or irrigation project or a construction project. Similarly in the case of the Inca Empire, there were specific job assignments for craftsmen and others working on the various kinds of construction projects, on the terracing of hillsides, and on the water-conduit system, and for the *yanacuna* and the *chasquis*. And in both countries, there were doubtless specific job assignments for other craftsmen, sculptors, for example.

(3) In Egypt, the economy provided the fellahin with a level of living that was kept low by taxes in kind on what they raised. The Inca Empire kept the level of living of farm people and herdsmen low by the allotments they were given and by the *mita* taxes levied on them. There were other people whom it seemed appropriate to provide with a significantly better level of living. In both countries, this included the skilled

craftsmen and, in the Inca Empire, also, the *yanacuna* and the Virgins of the Sun. At the top of the social ladder in both countries were nobles and priests. Some of these were perhaps in a position to fix the level of living they chose to enjoy.

In neither country was the total annual output all always consumed. In Egypt, there were years in which public officials were able to hold some of the output of grain and other things over as a reserve for the future. Inca officals apparently planned such a carryover every year.

Inca officials engaged in one type of economic planning for which there was no counterpart in the case of Egypt; they planned the take over of new territories. It is quite possible that there was a regular staff concerned with this planning and with other activities connected with such take overs, a staff that operated now on one new territory, now on another. There may, indeed, have been need for a corps of itinerant construction workers to build a palace for the governor and a Temple of the Sun in each major city, to construct highways and bridges, and to terrace hillsides.

Chapter IV

Developments in Military Technology and Government Organization in the Ancient Near East

Introduction

The history of the ancient Near East up to the time of Alexander the Great records a baffling succession of kings; some of whom like Urukagina were concerned to promote the welfare of the common man,[1] some like Tiglath Pileser III who were appallingly cruel.[2] Also, this history records that the scene shifts disconcertingly from one city-state or country to another.

The purpose of this essay is to explore the developments in the technology of warfare and related developments in government organization that help to explain why the scene shifts in such a kaleidoscopic fashion. We shall be only incidentally concerned with events in the lives of individual kings.

Probably it is obvious that, repeatedly, the rise of a kingdom to greatness was in large measure a reflection of its attainment to military superiority, and that this often came about by virtue of its priority in the acquisition of some new weapon or in the adoption of some new fighting technique. But no one seems to have traced such priorities systematically. We attempt to do this here, piecing out our account at points with surmises about things like an increase in the height and thickness of city walls or in the size and weight of battering-rams. Veblen made a suggestive comment "On the Merits of Borrowing" that seems applicable at least in some cases to a shift of scene induced by the acquisition of an improvement in military technology by a relatively backward kingdom that had the effect of giving it military pre-eminence. He said of the passing of a technique from one cultural situation to another, "The borrowed elements of industrial efficiency would be stripped of their fringe of conventional inhibitions." As compared to the community from which they came, "the borrowing community would be in a position to use them . . . with a better chance of utilising them to their full capacity." Clearly Veblen had in mind a culture sequence in which, initially, the community in which the about-to-be-borrowed culture trait originated was technologically more advanced than the community that was about to borrow it and in which, presently, the borrowing community proved to be able to make more effective use of the trait than the community that originated it had made. We shall have occasion to consider a number of communities each of which, in turn, borrowed something from a technologically more advanced community and succeeded in making a good thing of the borrowing.[3]

What made a particular kingdom the dominant military power at any particular time was partly the superiority of the military technology. But dominance was commonly also a matter of size. Developments in the technique of government organization and in a kingdom's communication system made possible a larger and larger dominant kingdom. After 2500 B.C., the dominant kingdom in the Fertile Crescent and Anatolia was always much larger than any of its competitors, when there was a clearly dominant kingdom. Developments in government organization are somewhat more difficult to trace than developments in military technology. But it seems desirable to do what we can to trace them.

We have divided our inquiry into seven topics as follows: I. We shall consider first the early dynastic period in Sumer. This included all but the last three hundred years of the third millennium B.C. It was a period in which various culture traits we think of as essentials of civilization developed or had quite recently developed: writing and reading, building large buildings and effective irrigation works, working metals and manufacturing metal products. We shall be mainly concerned with Sumerian military technology and Sumerian government.

II. In Section 2 we shall be dealing with the first three great empires the world has known, that of Agade, founded by the Akkadian, Sargon the Great, c. 2311 B.C.; that of the third dynasty of Ur, founded by Ur-Nammu, c. 2112 B.C.; and the Old Babylonian Empire. Hammurabi, an Amorite, ascended the throne of Babylon c. 1792 B.C., but he was some thirty years in building up his empire. The Akkadians borrowed almost all of the Sumerian culture, the Babylonians a very large part of it. Between the collapse of the Agade Empire c. 2193 and 2112 B.C., there was a short interregnum period. Between 2004 B.C., when the Elamites sacked Ur, and 1792 B.C., there was a longer interregnum.

We shall try to say something about the whys of this succession of empires.

III. Since our concern focuses on military technology and the relations between technological developments and developments in government organization, we propose to ignore the early history of Egypt. During the first three dynasties, a great civilization had come into being there, including a written language, the construction of great pyramids, and the construction of a system of catch basins and irrigation works along the Nile. But during most of these early years and until about 1730 B.C. Egyptians had paid little or no attention to developments in Mesopotamia and the Fertile Crescent.

One of them was the development of a new kind of army or army unit that we shall need to consider. We shall refer to it as a chariot-cavalry force. A people known as the Hyksos had a fairly large chariot-cavalry force. Starting from Palestine, c. 1730 B.C., with this force they invaded Egypt and conquered the country without fighting any real battle. It was a little more than a century before the Egyptians were able to expel the invaders.

Other peoples in the Fertile Crescent and Asia Minor made extensive use of this new kind of army unit, notably the Mitannians and the Hittites. The Mitannians had a very effective chariot-cavalry force. However, they do not seem to have learned enough from the Babylonians about other aspects of their civilization to do anything of consequence for our presnt inquiry. The Hittites certainly had. And they improved on the ways of doing things that they had borrowed. One significant innovation they introduced had to do with army organization. And one day, probably early in the sixteenth century B.C., King Mursilis led his army into Babylon and sacked the city.

IV. Thus far, we have been concerned only with land-warfare operations. Early seagoing vessels seem all to have been merchantmen. There was a type of vessel used extensively during much of the third millennium B.C. for carrying lumber from Lebanon to Egypt that was called a Byblos ship. It may sometimes have been used for piracy.

The first warship we hear about was a Greek vessel called a penteconter. It had twenty-five rowers on each side. It was used in the expedition against Troy, perhaps about 1200 B.C.

Probably early in the first millennium B.C., a bireme was developed. Quite possibly it was the Phoenicians who invented this type of vessel. Triremes superseded about 500 B.C. Both the Phoenician mercenaries and the Greeks had triremes in the battle of Salamis, 480 B.C.

In general, we shall not consider developments after the death of Alexander the Great in 323 B.C. In the case of warships, we shall make an exception. Triremes were superseded by more complicated vessels. During the First Punic War, both the Carthaginians and the Romans had quinqueremes with perhaps five men at each oar.

The Phoenicians never became rulers of a great empire; but they played a major role in various developments in navigation and communication. To make a place for comments on

67

these developments, we append a note to Chapter IV on Phoenician economic history.

V. This section is devoted to the Assyrian Empire. In the second millenium B.C., Assyria was just one of a number of relatively small city-states. During the ninth century B.C., it included all of Mesopotamia and a good deal of the rest of the Fertile Crescent, and it exacted tribute from places it did not attempt to rule. The Assyrians borrowed most of their civilization from the Babylonians and the Hittites. Their army included a chariot-cavalry force modeled on that of the Hittites. It was the first major army to have a cavalry division proper. There was both light and heavy infantry. There was a very effective engineering corps and probably a well-organized quartermaster corps. Tiglath Pileser III (c. 744–727 B.C.) made improvements in government organization. He took steps to make the local lords, who had largely ruled rural districts, more responsive to the crown. The newer parts of the Empire were divided into provinces; he appointed governors to govern them. He established an inspector system to check on the local lords and the province governors. He improved the Empire's messenger service. But heavy reliance continued to be placed on the fear the conquered peoples had of the cruelties of their conquerors. And Tiglath Pileser inaugurated an extensive resettlement program; thousands of people were evicted from their native habitats and made to settle in distant places. A very creditable aspect of Assyrian rule was the extensive construction programs undertaken by the Empire between c. 717 and 669 B.C. The Empire collapsed about 612 B.C.

VI. Two men collaborated to bring about the end of the Assyrian Empire, Cyaxares, king of the Medes, and Nabopolassar, who had just established a new dynasty in Babylon. Nebuchadrezzar, the son of Nabopolassar, married the daughter of Cyaxares. For a short time, he ruled an empire that included more territory than the Old Babylonian Empire had c. 547 B.C. Cyrus II, King of Persia, began a series of consquests that shortly made him the ruler of the greatest empire the world had so far known. His army had a particularly powerful cavalry force. His empire included a part of India. As a ruler, Cyrus cultivated the good will of his subjects.

In 521 B.C., Darius I ascended the throne. Under him, the Persians developed an extremely effective form of government organization. The Empire was divided into twenty provinces called satrapies. Each satrap ruled a semi-independent kingdom. He had a small military force and was a kind of vassal of the king. He collected taxes. The main army belonged to the king. The Empire had an extensive system of roads and a very efficient postal messenger service. Darius wanted to conquer Greece. An expedition he had spent against Greece in 490 B.C. was defeated at Marathon. His son, Xerxes, led a second expedition that was defeated at Salamis in 480 B.C. Despite these defeats Persia continued to have a great Empire.

VII. When Alexander the Great set out on his expedition against the Persians in 334 B.C. its alleged purpose was to wreak vengeance on them for the way Xerxes had desecrated Greek temples and sanctuaries in 481 B.C. He may have had more than vengeance in mind, for he took with him surveyors, a geographer, an historian, and an architect.

After he won the battle of the Granicus, he led his army south, taking one place after another. Perhaps by the time he had won the battle of Issus in 333 B.C., more certainly after he had won the battle of Arbela about two years later, Alexander had decided that he was engaged in an expedition to establish a great empire. He had to appoint someone to govern each piece of territory he conquered, and he could not afford to appoint many of the officers of his army. He needed them in his army. In 331 he appointed Mazaeus, the Persian general who had opposed him at Arbela, satrap of Babylonia. Thereafter he appointed other Persians to rule other satrapies. In India, he made each of two rival rajas the ruler of a substantial area. To help maintain the empire he was building, in 328 B.C., he married the daughter of a Sogdian baron, and in 324 B.C., he married Barsine, a daughter of Darius III. In the early days of his expedition, Alexander had a serious financial problem. This was presently solved by the gold and silver he captured.

In 330 and 329 B.C., he captured a vast hoard at Susa, Persepolis, and Pasargadae.

Much of the responsibility for the success of Alexander's expedition belongs to his corps of engineers and his quartermaster corps. We shall be somewhat concerned with the contributions made by these two noncombat units of his army. In India, east of Lahore on the Beas River, in 326 B.C., the army mutinied. Reluctantly, Alexander agreed to lead his men back westward. In 323 B.C., in Babylon he contracted a fever and died.

Notes

Introduction

1. Samuel N. Kramer, *The Sumerians: Their History, Culture and Character* (Chicago: University of Chicago Press, 1963), pp. 75, 79–83; *Encyclopaedia Britannica*, 1968, vol. 2, p. 961.

2. Georges Roux, *Ancient Iraq* (Harmondsworth, Middlesex, England: Penguin Books, 1966; first published by George Allen & Unwin, 1964) p. 278; Chester G. Starr, *A History of the Ancient World* (New York: Oxford University Press, 1965), p. 133.

3. Thorstein Veblen, *Imperial Germany and the Industrial Revolution* (New York: Macmillan Co., 1915), pp. 17, 36.

Section I. The Early Dynastic Period

For perhaps five hundred years during the third millennium B.C., quite possibly for a somewhat longer period, the Sumerians were technologically the most advanced people in the world. Their origin is obscure; they may have been Indo-Europeans. Probably, their technological innovation that had the most far-reaching effects was the development of the cuneiform script, the world's first full-fledged system of writing.

Interculture comparisons of economies necessarily have a less firm objective basis than interculture comparisons of technologies. But in this period the Sumerians had also an economic system that can reasonably be characterized as more advanced than that of any other contemporary culture area. The Sumerians had a very extensive division of labor; they had a monetary system, a wage system, and a price system; they engaged in buying and selling and in lending and borrowing transactions, all this long before there were any such economic institutions and economic activities elsewhere.[1]

Our present concern is with implements of war, with methods of warfare, and with government organization. In these areas as in much else the Sumerians were pioneers. In particular, they can fairly be said to have invented both the chariot and the phalanx formation for heavily armed infantry.

A panel of mosaic in shell and lapis lazuli that has come to be known as the *Standard of Ur* gives a good deal of information about early Sumer. This *Standard* was found by Sir C. Leonard Woolley in a royal grave at Ur. It pictures both infantry and chariots. The date of the grave is uncertain, perhaps before 3000 B.C.[2]

We learn from the *Standard* and other information that the early chariot it pictures was a heavy vehicle drawn by four draft animals—probably onagers—that were driven side by side. Control of the animals seems to have been effected by attaching the reins to a ring passed through the upper lip or the nasal septum of each of them. Each of the chariot's four wheels was made of two solid pieces of wood that were clamped

71

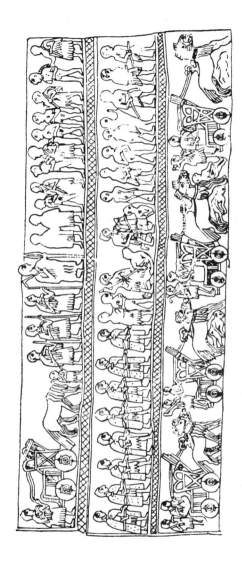

The mosaic Standard at Ur. One side, showing the Sumerian army of the fourth millennium B.C. *British Museum.*

together and fixed to the axle. The axle revolved with the wheels. The wheels had leather tires. The body of the carriage consisted of the bottom and three sides of a wooden box, the front side being carried upward in the form of two round-topped shields. Between these the reins were passed. Each chariot carried a driver and a fighting man. The latter was armed with four spears, two that could be projected with a throwing thong, two for close combat. The picture on the *Standard* shows a fighting contingent of four chariots.[3]

The middle picture on the *Standard* shows eight soldiers standing in a formation. Sir Leonard calls this formation a phalanx. This seems a very reasonable interpretation of the picture. Doubtless the phalanx formation at this time was in the early stages of development. The men wore copper helmets, kilts made perhaps of leather, and long heavy cloaks. They were armed with short spears or pikes with copper heads. In front of this phalanx, the picture shows skirmishers. These men were perhaps armed with axes, spears, daggers, or scimitars. The picture shows no bowmen, but it seems likely that the army at this time included them.[4]

When Eannatum was king of Lagash (c. 2380 B.C.), the chariot was no longer a major piece of offensive military apparatus. It was apparently reserved for the use of the king. At this time there may have been two-wheeled as well as four-wheeled chariots, the two-wheeled chariots being used by the king, the four-wheeled vehicles used for transporting equipment.[5]

By this time, too, the army's heavy infantry formation had been developed into a full-fledged phalanx. Eannatum's *Stele of the Vultures* shows a formation of six ranks of men wearing copper helmets and armed with heavy pikes and axes. The men in the front rank carried big rectangular shields.[6]

Probably by the twenty-sixth century B.C., each of the principal Sumerian cities had a wall around it. The wall around Erech (or Uruk or Warka) is said to have been six miles long and to have had over nine hundred towers. It was girdled by a moat. Legend had it that this wall was built by Gilgamesh,

73

the hero of the great Sumerian epic. The wall of each city enclosed the city proper and required anyone who would enter it to pass through one of its several gates. The urban area outside the city wall commonly included farms, gardens, and cattle folds and a harbor and commercial section in which business with foreigners was transacted.[7]

The central government of Sumer during the early dynastic period, when there was one, took the form of a hegemony among a group of city-states. The ruler of each of them, except the one in which the hegemony was vested, was a kind of king or perhaps better, a vassal of the ruler of the dominant city-state who was called a *lugal*. The vassal was called an *ensi*. The hegemony passed from one city-state to another. At various times it was vested in Kish, Ur, Lagash, Erech, Umma, and Adab.[8]

Most Sumerian military operations during the early dynastic period did not go far afield. There were battles between neighboring city-states competing for Sumerian hegemony; the winner in such a conflict might get tribute and booty from the loser. Also, there were actions by and against non-Sumerian forces; in such actions, the Sumerian aim was to drive or keep the foreigners out of Sumer. Before 2600 B.C., we have little factual information. There is some reason to think that for a time a horde of Elamites ruled at least a part of Sumer.[9]

Beginning with Lugalannemundu, who was king of Adab sometime during the twenty-sixth century B.C., we have a fairly definite record of Sumerian hegemonies. Not long after 2500 B.C., Mesilim was king of Kish, and for a while, Kish was the dominant Sumerian city. Ur-Nanshe established himself as king of Lagash c. 2450 B.C., and Lagash assumed the hegemony. He was followed on the throne of Lagash by his son and then by his grandson Eannatum. Eannatum was engaged in wars with Umma and other Sumerian cities and also with the Elamites. His brother and then his brother's son, Entemena, succeeded him. There was more trouble with Umma. Whether Lagash continued to have Sumerian hegemony at this time is not clear. Entemena's immediate successors were first his son, Enannatum II, next Enetarzi, and after him Lugalanda. Then followed Urukagina, who sought to put into effect a great social reform program. He was shortly oousted and the city sacked by Lugalzaggesi, who had become *ensi* of Umma. Lugalzaggesi was conquered by an Akkadian, Sargon the Great, c. 2300 B.C.[10]

Despite the absence of a real central government in Sumer, and despite the transfers of hegemony from one city-state to another, Sumerian culture dominated not only Mesopotamia but also about the whole of the Fertile Crescent. This was so throughout the early dynastic period, and it continued to be pretty much so for the next two thousand years. No doubt an important factor in Sumerian dominance during the pre-Sargon period was the superiority of the military forces of the city-states. If this did not bring much in the way of national unity, it did provide enough peace to facilitate a very substantial increase in industrial production in Sumer and in intercommunity trade throughout an area rather wider than the Fertile Crescent.

Notes

Section I

1. In respect to technological and economic development, Egypt was not a serious competitor. She had no wheeled vehicles before 1800 B.C. At that time she was not using the arch, dome, or vault in building construction. During the third millennium B.C., she was slower in developing metallurgy and the potter's wheel. The development of her hieroglyphic script seems to have come appreciably later than development of writing in Sumer. In 2200 B.C., she was still essentially a nonmoney economy. On Egypt, see John A. Wilson, *The Culture of Ancient Egypt* (Chicago: University of Chicago Press, 1951), pp. 37–38, 50, 82–84; Chester G. Starr, *A History of Ancient Worlds* (New York: Oxford University Press, 1965), p. 55. On Sumer, see Samuel N. Kramer, *The Sumerians: Their History, Culture and Character* (Chicago: University of Chicago Press, 1963), pp. 61, 79, 83–88, 93, 101–8; C. Leonard Woolley, *The Sumerians* (London: Oxford University Press, 1928; reprint ed., New York: W. W. Norton & Co., 1965) pp. 117–18; Georges Roux, *Ancient Iraq* (Harmondsworth, Middlesex, England: Penguin Books, 1966; first published by George Allen & Unwin, 1964), 158, 198; A. Leo Oppenheim, *Ancient Mes-*

opotamia: *Portrait of a Dead Civilization* (Chicago: University of Chicago Press, 1964), pp. 86–87, 307.

2. See cut. This is a photographic reproduction of p. 51 of C. Leonard Woolley's book, *The Sumerians*. Woolley says the *Standard* "dates from about 3500 B.C." We think later than that.

3. Woolley, *The Sumerians*, pp. 50, 52; V. Gordon Childe, *Social Evolution* (New York: Schuman, 1951), pp. 124–25, 718, 720–21; O.R. Gurney, *The Hittites* (Baltimore: Penguin Books, 1952), p. 104.

4. Woolley, *The Sumerians*, p. 53–54.

5. Ibid., p. 55.

6. Ibid., p. 56.

7. Starr, *Ancient World*, pp. 32–33; Oppenheim, *Ancient Mesopotamia*, p. 116; *Encyclopaedia Britannica*, 1968, vol. 8, p. 671.

8. Roux, *Ancient Iraq*, p. 125.

9. Ibid., p. 130.

10. Kramer, *Sumerians*, pp. 51–59.

Section II. The Sargon–Ur III–Hammurabi Era

It will be convenient to treat the years from c. 2311 to 1595 B.C. as a single era, although this long period involves a considerable diversity of events. It includes the rise and fall of the empire established by Sargon the Great at Agade (also written Akkad—he was an Akkadian) c. 2371–c. 2255; the Third Dynasty of Ur c. 2112 to c. 2004; and the rise and fall of the empire established by the Amorite, Hammurabi, at Babylon, c. 1792 to c. 1595 B.C. Between the Agade Empire and Ur III there was a brief period of disorder in which Mesopotamia was overrun by the Gutians. Between Ur III and Hammurabi there was a more complicated interregnum.

The first remarkable achievement of Sargon was a palace revolution. He had been cupbearer to Ur-Zababa, King of Kish; he took over the kingship c. 2371 B.C. Not long after this he made a surprise attack on Erech. He succeeded in capturing the city, and he took King Lugalzaggesi a prisoner. Lugalzaggesi had been not only king of Erech but also *lugal* of Sumer. We do not know that Sargon had any special advantages that helped him in this operation. It is just possible that he had bronze weapons, while the armed forces defending Erech had only copper weapons. Bronze was replacing copper at about this time.[1]

Next, Sargon captured three great Sumerian cities, one after another, Ur, Lagash, and Umma. We are not told about the battles this involved. Quite possibly there were no battles. In fact, we suspect that he took each of these cities by a carefully planned wall-scaling operation. If each of them was taken by surprise in this way, only the small force that scaled the city's wall may have been needed to capture it. About the city walls, we are told merely that when he had taken a city, he destroyed its walls.[2]

To demonstrate the greatness he had achieved, Sargon founded, on the Euphrates not far from Kish, a new capital city, Agade. It shortly became a very prosperous and resplendent urban seaport community.[3]

77

Sargon spent a good deal of time during the early years of his long reign (c. 2371 to 2316 B.C.) in expeditions of conquest. He went west and north as far as Lebanon and the Taurus range. Among the cities he captured were Mari and apparently Nineveh. He also led an expedition eastward into Elam. We know almost nothing about his army. There is no reason to think it was a very large one. We can be quite sure it was small enough so that he had no problem of provisioning it; his men simply lived off the land.[4]

During his later years he had repeatedly to lead an army to put down a revolt. And after his death his successors, his son Rimush, his son Manishtushu, and his grandson Naram-Sin, had various revolts to put down.[5]

The rule of Sargon and his successors involved problems because they were Akkadians, and Akkadians were Semites and foreigners, neighborly foreigners perhaps, but still foreigners. Sargon appointed an Akkadian as governor of each of the principal cities, and several cities had Akkadian garrisons. But he was anxious that what he did should in important ways conform to Sumerian customs. He had his daughter made a priestess in the temple of Nanna at Ur. And he called himself "anointed priest of Anu" and "great *ensi* of Enlil." He and both his sons, Rimush and Manishtushu, commemorated their victories by erecting statues of themselves in Enlil's temple at Nippur.[6]

The Akkadians had no separate culture of their own. Long before Sargon, they had borrowed, with one major exception, practically the whole of Sumerian culture. They took over Sumerian technology in its entirety. They adopted the Sumerians' religion and mythology and their pantheon. They plagiarized Sumerian literature. And the Sumerian economy was expanded into a Sumero-Akkadian economy. The major exception was language. They developed a cuneiform script in which they wrote Akkadian.[7]

The Agade Empire may be said to have ended with the death of Naram-Sin, Sargon's grandson, c. 2255 B.C. It is true that Sharkalisharri, Naram-Sin's son, continued to occupy the throne at Agade until he died c. 2230 B.C., but by that time much of the empire had seceded. Before 2255 B.C., it had been held together by the military power of the great generals who headed it. When it was headed by a man like Sharkalisharri, who was not a great general, it simply fell apart. The great generals had built up a huge palace organization, but they did not have much in the way of an empire government.[8]

The invaders who destroyed Agade were probably Gutians, a warlike people from the Zagros Mountains whom the Sumero-Akkadians did not consider civilized. They appear to have dominated a good deal of Mesopotamia for seventy-odd years following the death of Naram-Sin. We do not know just when Agade was destroyed, but the destruction was extremely complete. No archeologist has been able to identify any part of the remains of the city.[9]

Utuhegal, *ensi* of Erech, defeated the Gutians in battle c. 2120 B.C. and captured Tiriqan, their king, thus liberating Sumer and Akkad.[10]

Seven years later, Ur-Nammu, governor of Ur, evicted Utuhegal and established the Third Dynasty of Ur. He shortly built up a great empire. It presently included most of Sumer and Elam and a good deal of Syria and Lebanon; it was at least as large as the Agade Empire. The Sumerians developed for it an effective form of central government. In a number of cities, the *ensis* as well as the high priests were appointees of the king, some of them appointees who had been shifted from one city to another. The *ensis* and, likewise, the provincial governors in places like Mari, Susa in Elam, and Assur in Assyria were visited regularly by royal inspectors. There was a royal courier system for transmitting messages, orders and reports.[11]

At the local government level there was less change from the Agade and earlier periods. Local court administration continued to be vested in the city assembly, and the assembly continued to advise on local public works. But the principal local government functions continued to be in the hands of the *ensi*. His responsibilities included public works, the collection of taxes, and the maintenance of law and order. His administration seems to have been more closely supervised than it had been under the Agade Empire.[12]

The Third Dynasty of Ur was a period in which there was a great deal of construction work. Walls were built around the city that were said to be as high as a mountain. It is reasonable to suppose that it had become the practice to make a city's walls so high that unless they could be breached, the city could not be taken without a siege. The construction work included a good many temples and roads and irrigation systems as well as city walls. Fortresses were built along the main highways. They were staffed with imperial police forces that protected not only the royal couriers from marauders but also merchants and their caravans that were travelling from one part of the empire to another. This policing system facilitated a substantial growth in intercommunity trade and an increase in industrial production. There was an accompanying increase in population and probably an improvement in the average level of living.[13]

The growth in business and financial activities in the cities during the latter part of the third millennium B.C. had as a necessary accompaniment a development of business common law. Ur-Nammu put together what has come to be known as his "Code of Law." It was mainly a summary of the court decisions that had accumulated in his time; the practice of *stare decisis* seems to have been followed in most cases. But his "Code" was concerned not only with court decisions but also with establishing a system of honest and standard weights and measures.[14]

The Ur III period was by no means entirely peaceful. Ur-Nammu was probably killed in a battle with the Gutians. He was succeeded by his son, Shulgi, whose wife seems to have been an Akkadian, and by his grandson, Amar-Sin. Both Shulgi and Amar-Sin spent a good deal of time in fighting battles; Shu-Sin, the brother of Amar-Sin, ascended the throne c. 2038 B.C. By this time, a nomadic people from Syria, the Amorites, had become extremely troublesome. Somewhere be-

80

tween Mari and Ur, he built a fortress to keep these barbaric people in check. The fortress seems to have served its purpose effectively for some ten years. In 2029 B.C. he died and was succeeeded by his son, Ibbi-Sin. During Ibbi-Sin's reign, the empire disintegrated. In his second year, Eshnunna seceded; in his third, Susa. The imperial police force proved unable to hold the Amorites in check. To relieve the famine conditions that had developed in Ur, Ibbi-Sin sent one of his generals, Ishbi-Erra, to buy grain in Nippur and Isin. In a letter to the king Ishbi-Erra reported that he had bought the grain, but that he was holding it at Isin because the Amorites had cut off the roads to Ur. He asked to be put in charge of Isin and Nippur, which he said the Amorites were threatening. Ibbi-Sin agreed. In 2017 B.C., Ishbi-Erra proclaimed himself king of Isin; at that time, he controlled Nippur and was extending his control elswewhere in Mesopotamia. In 2006 B.C., the Elamites besieged Ur; in 2004, they sacked it and Ibbi-Sin was taken prisoner.[15]

During much of its first seventy-five years, the Ur III Empire seemed to be so well organized that it could be expected to last a great many years. Hindsight makes clear that it needed a police force that could do a good deal more than suppress the activities of individual marauders. It needed a police force that could defeat a rebellious armed force. We do not know why Eshnunna, Susa, Isin, and apparently other cities came to desire to secede. Possibly the imperial inspectors failed to promote good will toward the Emperor, as they should have. In any case, there is probably no sure way to protect a ruler against a traitorous act by one of his subordinates.

During the interregnum that followed the fall of the Ur III Empire, Isin became the dominant Sumerian city. While he was king of Isin (c. 1934–1924), Lipit-Ishtar wrote a "Code of Law." During the next hundred-odd years, several non-Sumerian cities became extremely important, especially Eshnunna, Mari, Assur, and Babylon. While Bilalama was king of Eshnunna, he wrote a "Code of Law"; he and Lipit-Ishtar seem to have been contemporaries. After Lipit-Ishtar, Isin seems to have been in difficulties; after Bilalama, there were difficulties, also, for Eshnunna.[16]

For a time Mari and Assur were friendly rivals. Iahdum-Lim, king of Mari, led a successful military expedition westward to the Mediterranean that seems to have stimulated action on the part of Assyria. Not much later, Iahdum-Lim was murdered. Shamshi-Adad, king of Assur, c. 1814 to 1782 B.C., took advantage of the situation to capture Mari. Thus he established what has sometimes been called the first Assyrian Empire.[17]

When Hammurabi ascended the throne of Babylon c. 1792 B.C., the kingdom he had inherited was still a small one. Shamshi-Adad treated him courteously; but, of course, Assur and Babylon were rivals. Hammurabi spent the first five years of his reign making sure of his position; during the next five, he captured a good deal of Sumer. Then for a number of years, he devoted himself to building temples and fortifications. In the twenty-ninth year of his reign, a combined force from Elam, Eshnunna, Assur, and Gutium attacked Babylon. Hammurabi defeated them. During the next several years, he did a good deal of fighting; nearly all of Mesopotamia—including a part of Assyria—was added to his empire. We think, however, that his empire never included any territory in Syria or Phoenicia, and perhaps none in Elam, although his influence was surely felt in these areas.[18]

Hammurabi, like Sargon, was careful to observe Sumerian religious practices although, by this time, the Semitic peoples, Akkadians and Amorites, had almost completely swamped the Sumerian people. In a good many Sumerian cities "including Nippur, the temples were rebuilt, repaired or embellished in the true Mesopotamian royal tradition." But Hammurabi had the Epic of Creation rewritten by his priests to give Marduk, the tutelary deity of Babylon, the leading role.[19]

We are not told much about the way what has come to be known as the Old Babylonian Empire was organized. Each of the principal cities and the area around it continued to be governed by an *ensi*. Groupings of cities apparently constituted provinces, each province being governed by a provincial governor. We can safely assume that there were imperial inspectors who supervised the *ensis* and the provincial governors as closely as the inspectors of the Ur III Empire had, and that they may have been more tactful about the way they did it. We can safely assume also that the Empire had an efficient courier service.[20]

Hammurabi had a "Code of Law" that has been fully preserved to us. Like its predecessors, it was to some extent a summary of common law; also, it included statutory edicts. Among these were provisions concerned with the fixing of various wage rates, fees, prices, and interest rates. The Hammurabi "Code" seems to have pushed in the direction of promoting intercity uniformity. Its penalties were more severe than those of the Ur-Nammu "Code" and were more on an eye-for-an-eye basis. Also, there was more extensive use of the death penalty and of punishment by mutilation.[21]

What the Sumerians and the Babylonians had in the way of mathematics is only remotely related to developments in military technology and government organization, but we propose to digress to say something about this. The Sumerians had a place notation for writing numbers that enabled them to make significant developments in arithmetic, algebra, and geometry. They had tables useful for making various calculations, among them tables of squares and square roots, cubes and cube roots, sums of squares, and reciprocals. The Babylonians pushed forward. By 1700 B.C., they apparently knew the Pythagorean theorem and various formulas for calculating areas. For the area of a circle they took $3.125r^2$ as an approximation. They had techniques for solving a number of problems involving quadratic equations.[22]

The Babylonians, like the Akkadians, simply took over Sumerian culture. They also adopted the Akkadian language. But in various fields, architecture and metal work as well as mathematics, they improved on what they had borrowed. Apparently, however, they introduced no significant improvement in military technology. To their failure to keep abreast of developments in this area, we shall, in the next chapter, attribute the end of the Old Babylonian Empire.[23]

Notes

Section II.

1. Samuel M. Kramer, *The Sumerians: Their History, Culture and Character* (Chicago: University of Chicago Press, 1963), pp. 60, 103; Georges Roux, *Ancient Iraq* (Harmondsworth, Middlesex, England: Penguin Books, 1966; first published by George Allen & Unwin, 1964), p. 141; C. Leonard Woolley, *The Sumerians* (London: Oxford University Press, 1928; reprint ed., New York: W. W. Norton & Co., 1965), p. 73; *Encyclopaedia Britannica*, 1968, vol. 15, p. 233.

2. Kramer, *Sumerians*, p. 60; Roux, *Ancient Iraq*, p. 141.

3. Kramer, *Sumerians*, p. 61; Roux, *Ancient Iraq*, p. 141.

4. Kramer, *Sumerians*, pp. 60–61; Roux, *Ancient Iraq*, pp. 141–43.

5. Kramer, *Sumerians*, p. 61; Roux, *Ancient Iraq*, p. 143.

6. Kramer, *Sumerians*, pp. 59, 61, 288; Roux, *Ancient Iraq*, p. 141; Woolley, *The Sumerians*, pp. 77, 80, 83.

7. Kramer, *Sumerians*, p. 291; Roux, *Ancient Iraq*, p. 140; Woolley, *The Sumerians*, pp. 65, 77, 79.

8. Kramer, *Sumerians*, p. 68; Roux, *Ancient Iraq*, p. 146.

9. Kramer, *Sumerians*, pp. 61, 62, 66, 68; Roux, *Ancient Iraq*, p. 147; Woolley, *The Sumerians*, p. 83; A. Leo Oppenheim, *Ancient Mesopotamia: Portrait of a Dead Civilization* (Chicago: University of Chicago Press, 1964), p. 154.

10. Kramer, *Sumerians*, pp. 67–68; Roux, *Ancient Iraq*, p. 149.

11. Kramer, *Sumerians*, p. 68; Roux, *Ancient Iraq*, pp. 149–50, 156, 157; Woolley, *The Sumerians*, p. 138. The name of Ur-Nammu's son was formerly written "Dungi"; the name of Shulgi's son was formerly written "Bur-Sin." *Encyclopaedia Britannica*, 1968, vol. 2, p. 962.

12. Kramer, *Sumerians*, pp. 74, 78; Roux, *Ancient Iraq*, p. 157; Oppenheim, *Ancient Mesopotamia*, pp. 111–12.

13. Kramer, *Sumerians*, p. 68; Roux, *Ancient Iraq*, pp. 150–51, 156, 158, 160; Woolley, *The Sumerians*, pp. 132–35, 140; Oppenheim, *Ancient Mesopotamia*, pp. 117, 155; *Encyclopaedia Britannica*, 1968, vol. 2, p. 962.

14. Kramer, *Sumerians*, pp. 68, 83–85, 124; Roux, *Ancient Iraq*, p. 150.

15. Kramer, *Sumerians*, pp. 68–69, 70–71; Roux, *Ancient Iraq*, pp. 156, 157, 161–63; Woolley, *The Sumerians*, pp. 168–69; *Encyclopaedia Britannica*, 1968, vol. 2, p. 962.

16. Roux, *Ancient Iraq*, pp. 167, 170–71, 176–77.

17. Roux, *Ancient Iraq*, pp. 171–77.

18. Kramer, *Sumerians*, p. 72; Roux, *Ancient Iraq*, pp. 177–82; Oppenheim, *Ancient Mesopotamia*, pp. 156–57, 165.

19. Roux, *Ancient Iraq*, p. 183; Woolley, *The Sumerians*, p. 122; *Encyclopaedia Britannica*, 1929, vol. 11, p. 135.

20. Roux, *Ancient Iraq*, pp. 196–97, 183.

21. Roux, *Ancient Iraq*, pp. 184–88; Woolley, *The Sumerians*, pp. 91–93; Chester G. Starr, *A History of the Ancient World* (New York: Oxford University Press, 1965), pp. 47–48; *Encyclopaedia Britannica*, 1929, vol. 2, p. 862; vol. 11, p. 135; *Encyclopaedia Britannica*, 1968, vol. 2, p. 963; vol. 11, pp. 41–43; Kramer, *Sumerians*, pp. 87, 295.

22. Kramer, *Sumerians*, pp. 91–93; Oppenheim, *Ancient Mesopotamia*, pp. 306–7; O. Neugebauer, "Ancient Mathematics and Astronomy," in *A History of Technology*, eds. Charles Singer, E. J. Holmyard, and A. R. Hall (New York: Oxford University Press, 1954), vol. 1, p. 790; *Encyclopaedia Britannica*, 1968, vol. 14, p. 1104.

23. Kramer, *Sumerians*, p. 291.

Section III. The Hyksos and the Hittites

During the second millenium B.C. three peoples who lived in the part of Asia to the west and north of the Old Babylonian Empire became important: the Hyksos, the Mitannians, and the Hittites. Each of them became important, in part at least, because they were skilled horsemen. Each of these peoples was a hybrid of the old inhabitants of the area they occupied and newcomers who were Indo-Europeans. In each of these culture areas, the Indo-Europeans became the dominant class.[1]

Each of these peoples adopted Babylonian technology. Each used the cuneiform script to write their language. Each was skilled in making bronze and in manufacturing bronze articles, including weapons. Each seem to have made use of a new offensive military device, a battering-ram. And each used the horse as a draft animal. The Babylonians surely knew about battering-rams and about horses, but they do not seem to have made much use of either.[2]

The horse was probably domesticated by 3000 B.C. It was brought into Mesopotamia about 2000 B.C. and for a long time was used there only as a draft animal. The harness consisted of a simple bridle and a yoke and pole. The bridle included a bit; from the start a bit seems to have been used to control the animal, rather than a ring through his lip or nasal septum. The yoke was a wooden bar that rested on the necks of the two draft animals; horses seem to have been used at first only in teams. Straps that went around the neck of each horse and across his breast were fastened to the yoke. The pole at one end was strapped to the yoke; in the case of a chariot or wagon the other end was strapped to the axle. The reins went from the bridle through rings on the yoke to the driver.[3]

Somewhere in the area with which we are concerned, a new method of fighting and a new type of army unit was developed. The new army unit consisted of a large number of charioteers and fighting men mounted on a large number of light, maneuverable chariots. Since the Hyksos were the first people we know about to have had such a unit and make extensive use of it, we think it is reasonable to give them credit for developing it. We will call the new army unit a chariot-cavalry force.[4]

The name "Hyksos" is apparently a Greek corruption of an Egyptian term meaning "chieftains of a foreign hill-country." Most of the people this term covers were probably Semitic and spoke a Semitic language. The upper crust were Indo-Europeans. The Hyksos had a chariot-cavalry force of perhaps serveral thousand charioteers and chariots. Starting from Palestine, they invaded Egypt c. 1730 B.C. No doubt they chose Egypt as a country to conquer partly because of her wealth, partly because she had no up-to-date defenses, no walled cities. During the first twelve dynasties, the Egyptians, somewhat deliberately it would seem, had paid little or no attention to developments in the Fertile Crescent. The Hyksos conquered Egypt apparently without fighting a battle.[5]

The Hyksos founded a city in the Nile delta, Avaris (also called Tanis), and made this the capital of an empire that included Egypt and at least part of Palestine. They did not attempt to go very far south in Egypt. Apparently an Egyptian dynasty, or rather dynasties (there were several of them), in Thebes continued nominally to rule the country south of the delta area. The government in Thebes paid tribute to the Hyksos.[6]

The Hyksos chariots were two-wheeled. The wheels had spokes, probably six spokes per wheel. Each chariot had a crew of two men, the driver and a bowman. It was drawn by a team of two horses. The bowmen carried shields and apparently wore helmets and some kind of armor. John A. Wilson claims that they were equpped with improved bronze swords and laminated bows that shot particularly swift arrows.[7]

Not much else can be said about developments in war technology and tactics introduced by the Hyksos or their immediate predecessors. In fortifying their camps they put a glacis or agger around the walls as a defense against battering-rams.[8]

Domination of Egypt by the Hyksos continued for a little

over a century. They were expelled c. 1570 B.C. By that time the Egyptians had learned a great deal about the arts of warfare. They had an up-to-date chariot-cavalry force.[9] The Hyksos probably returned to Palestine. We hear no more about them. Beginning some time toward the end of the third millennium B.C. there seem to have been three successive hordes of Indo-Europeans that invaded Anatolia. The people known as Hittites were hybrids of these invaders, particularly the Nesites, and the older inhabitants. We propose to divide our comments on these people into two parts, one concerned with the Old Kingdom (c. 1680 to 1460 B.C.), the other with the Hittite Empire (c. 1460 until shortly after 1215 B.C.), and to sandwich in between these two parts a mention of the Kassite Dynasty in Babylon and two paragraphs on the Mitannians.

Labarnas I began his reign as king of the Hittites c. 1680 B.C. He was not the first ruler of this kingdom. His grandfather and father preceded him; but we know nothing about them except that their kingdom was small and that the principal officers under each of them were apparently the king's close relatives.[10]

No authentic inscription written by Labarnas I has survived, but one written later about his kingdom lists seven Hittite cities in eastern Anatolia and claims that Labarnas "made the seas his frontiers." Its capital was Kussera.[11]

His son, Labarnas II, moved the capital to Hattusas (also written Boghazköy) and changed his name to Hattusilis. The new capital had natural advantages that enabled him to make it a great fortress.[12]

The Hittites had borrowed extensively from the Babylonians and had adopted the new fighting technique. Their army included a powerful chariot-cavalry force. The kingdom was expanded somewhat further under Hattusilis, still further under his son, Mursilis I. Probably not long after 1600 B.C., King Mursilis I led his army on an expedition against Babylon. He captured and sacked the city, thus bringing the Old Babylonian Empire to an end.[13]

We do not know how Mursilis made his entry into Babylon.

The city's walls were probably too high for an escalade operation. He may simply have battered down the city's gates. Another possibility is suggested by the fact that the Euphrates ran through the city. We do not know how its entrance and egress were fortified; Mursilis may have found a way to get through one of these two openings in the city wall. Again, possibly he had help from people inside the city.[14]

In Babylon Mursilis was a long way from home. He had doubtless taken his expeditionary force down the Euphrates by boat, but much of the way he had had to come by land. Even if his army was just a chariot-cavalry force with no infantry, getting to Babylon must have taken some six weeks. He had no way of knowing what had been happening in Hattusas during all this time. He had been depending on the relatives he left in charge to look after things. Apparently he decided to start back immediately. In fact, he may have decided to hurry. He seems to have left by the wayside at Hana the statue of the great Babylonian god, Marduk, he had stolen from the temple.[15]

His concern about what had been going on in his absence at Hattusas was well grounded. He had scarcely returned to the city when he was assassinated by his brother-in-law, Hantilis. A period of turmoil followed. Telpinus, regarded by some as the last king of the Old Kingdom, ascended the throne c. 1525 B.C. He succeeded in establishing a firm government. The most significant event during his reign was the edict he promulgated that prescribed a precise law of succession.[16]

The Mitannians were a cross between a mountain people, probably from Armenia, and a dominant Indo-European group. The kingdom of Mitanni centered in northwestern Mesopotamia. Where its capital, Washukkanni, was located has not been determined; possibly it was on the upper Khabur river. The Mitannians had a powerful army that included a chariot-cavalry contingent. During the fifteenth century B.C. and part of the fourteenth, each king of Assur seems to have been a vassal of the king of Mitanni. During much of the fifteenth century there were repeated encounters between Egyptian and Mitannian military forces. During the last decade of that century there were very friendly relations between the two countries. Amenophis III (c. 1405–1367 B.C.) married the daughter of Shutarna, king of Metanni.[17]

In 1370 B.C., or not long after that, Suppiluliumas, king of the Hittites, hitherto unknown in this part of the world, led an expedition into Mitannian territory and against Aleppo, a great stronghold in Syria. At first he was unsuccessful, but presently he plundered Washukkanni and captured Aleppo. This alone would have been serious enough for Mitanni; but there were palace intrigues and quarrels about succession to the throne. King Tusgratta was murdered by his son, c. 1360 Then Ashur-uballit, king of Assur (c. 1365 to 1330), declared his independence. By 1350 B.C., the Mitannian kingdom had disintegrated.[18]

As a prelude to a consideration of the Hittite Empire, we should probably note that shortly after Mursilis sacked Babylon a new dynasty took over the rule of the city and of much of Mesopotamia, the Kassite Dynasty. The Kassites were a hybrid people, immigrant Indo-Euorpeans who interbred with and dominated people from the Zagros Mountains. Their not very distinguished rule extended over a period of some four hundred and thirty years.[19]

The first king of the Hittites during what is called the Empire Period was Tudhaliyas II (c. 1460 to 1440 B.C.). About him, we know only that he is said to have sacked Aleppo. We know nothing about his immediate successors. The kingdom seems to have been quite small until his great grandson, Suppiluliumas I, ascended the throne. Suppliluliumas was a great general. What his conquests added to the kingdom, including his expedition into Mitanni and Syria and his capture of Aleppo, made it an empire.[20]

Our primary concern, however, is not with King Suppiluliumas or any of the kings who followed him. It is with the Hittite military establishment and with other aspects of the Hittite culture. The might of the Empire's military establishment was doubtless in large part due to its chariot-cavalry force.

The Hittite chariots were slightly heavier than those of the Hyksos and the Egyptians, and they carried a three-man crew. Each charioteer apparently owned his chariot. If so, the charioteers must have been wealthy nobles, and the other members of the chariot crews may have been their personal servants. The Hittite chariot-cavalry force could move over a considerable distance in a comparatively short time and make a powerful surprise attack. Their accounts of their tactics make it clear that they often relied on catching the enemy unawares for the success of a military venture.[21]

In addition to their chariot-cavalry force, the Hittite army included a substantial infantry contingent. And it included not only fighting men but also auxiliary units. There was a rudimental engineering corps that handled construction of encampment fortifications and that presumably operated their heavy battering-rams. They were doubtless also responsible for building aggers. Another auxiliary unit that the Hittite army possessed was an embryonic quartermaster corps. This included pack asses and heavy four-wheeled wagons that carried supplies and camping equipment. They did not have what we would call a cavalry division; they did have messengers who were mounted on horseback. They seem to have been the first people to use the horse as a mount. And while they did not have a navy, they evidently had boats of some sort, for King Arnuwandas III (c. 1250 B.C.) considered Cyprus to be Hittite territory.[22]

Hittite cities during the Empire period were strongly fortified. At Hattusas, outside the main city wall about twenty feet in front of it, there was a lower subsidiary wall. The main wall consisted of an outer and an inner masonry shell, the space in between them being filled with rubble. Outside the subsidiary wall, there was at many places a scattering of large stones. The main wall was reinforced at intervals of one hundred feet or so by large towers that projected out from the wall. There were three gates; approach to each of them was up a steep ramp with a sharp turn. At one point, there was a tunnel under the wall through which the city defenders could make a sortie against attackers. Sentries posted on roads leading to the city may, at times, have been continuously on duty.[23]

The Hittites got the general plan for their city walls, like many other things, from the Babylonians, the two masonry shells with rubble in between and the protruding, reinforcing towers. However, in the masonry shell for the wall, or at least the lower part of it, they used native stone instead of Mesopotamian brick, huge stone blocks for the outer shell. And they doubtless added various novel features, including the secondary outside wall and the tunnel for sorties against an attacking enemy.

The written records that tell us about the Hittites go back to about the middle of the second millenium B.C. Their economy was largely rural, but there were a number of cities. As in Babylonia, there were skilled craftsmen of various types. The Hittites were especially noted for their metal work. They had a monetary system not very different from the Babylonian. Silver was the standard of value. There were forty (instead of sixty) shekels to one mina. Fragments of a law "code" found at Hattusas have been pieced together. There were some two hundred "laws." The matters dealt with were quite similar to those in the Hammurabi "Code." Many of them, to judge from their wording, were court-case precedents. But various prices, fees, and wage rates were prescribed. There was a more limited use of the death penalty and punishment by mutilation than in the Hammurabi "Code," and more emphasis was put on compensating the injured party, less on wreaking vengeance on the wrongdoer.[24]

The Hittites borrowed very extensively from other peoples, particularly from the Babylonians. A curious practice they took over was Babylonian methods of divination and interpreting omens. But there were distinctly original features of their culture, too. One of them was the bas-relief sculptures they carved on the blocks of stone that were integral parts of the lower portion of a palace wall. A particularly significant feature of their culture was the kingly custom of writing annals. The succession decree proclaimed by King Telipinus included a prefatory annals section. Other kings in the prefaces to decrees they promulgated followed his example. King Mursilis II simply wrote annals that provided an historical record of events during his reign, thus fully establishing the practice of writing annals.[25] The Hittite Empire was brought to an end c. 1200 B.C. by a horde of Indo-European invaders from the north who overran not only Anatolia but also northern Syria and Phoenicia. Thereafter, Hittite culture survived only in a few petty Neo-Hittite kingdoms in northern Syria and the Taurus area. Although many of the Hittite traditions were continued in these kingdoms, their language and their religion were not the language and religion of Hattusas, and they erected numerous stone monuments bearing hieroglyphic inscriptions.[26]

Notes

Section III.

1. Georges Roux, *Ancient Iraq* (Harmondsworth, Middlesex, England: Penguin Books, 1966; first published by George Allen & Unwin, 1964), pp. 202, 206–7, 208.

2. Ibid., p. 203.

3. *Encyclopaedia Britannica,* 1929, vol. 5, p. 247; *Encyclopaedia Britannica,* 1968, vol. 1, p. 979; vol. 11, p. 119; Xenophon, *Anabasis,* rev. ed., edited and with an introduction by William W. Goodwin and John Williams White; Greek-English dictionary by John Williams White and Morris H. Morgan (New York: Ginn & Co., 1894), pp. 92–93 of the dictionary.

4. *Encyclopaedia Britannica,* 1929, vol. 17, p. 566.

5. Chester G. Starr, *A History of the Ancient World* (New York: Oxford University Press, 1965), p. 88; John A. Wilson, *The Culture of Ancient Egypt* (Chicago: University of Chicago Press, 1951), pp. 159–61; Roux, *Ancient Iraq,* pp. 212, 216; A. Leo Oppenheim, *Ancient Mesopotamia: Portrait of a Dead Civilization* (Chicago: University of Chicago Press, 1964), p. 127; Cyrus H. Gordon, *The Ancient Near East,* rev. ed. (New York: W.W. Norton & Co., 1965; originally published as *The World of the Old Testament,* Ventnor Publishers, 1953), pp. 66, 180; *Encyclopaedia Britannica,* 1929, vol. 8, p. 71; *Encyclopaedia Britannica,* 1968, vol. 11, p. 893.

6. Roux, *Ancient Iraq,* pp. 216, 226; Gordon, *The Ancient Near East,* p. 66; Starr, *Ancient World,* p. 88; Wilson, *Ancient Egypt,* pp. 159–61; *Encyclopaedia Britannica,* 1929, vol. 8, pp. 63, 72; *Encyclopaedia Britannica,* 1968, vol. 8; pp. 35, 46; vol. 11, p. 893.

7. Starr, *Ancient World,* p. 89; Wilson, *Ancient Egypt,* pp. 161, 164; V.

Gordon Childe, "Rotary Motion" and "Wheeled Vehicles," in *A History of Technology*, eds. Charles Singer, E. J. Holmyard, and A. R. Hall (New York: Oxford University Press, 1954). It is here assumed that the Hyksos chariots, like those of the Egyptians, were two wheeled and that each had a crew of two and was drawn by a team of two horses; the Egyptians seem to have followed the Hyksos model.

8. Starr, *Ancient World*, p. 89.

9. Starr, *Ancient World*, p. 89; Gordon, *The Ancient Near East*, pp. 66–67; *Encyclopaedia Britannica*, 1968, vol. 8, pp. 35, 46, vol. 11, p. 893.

10. Roux, *Ancient Iraq*, p. 219; O. R. Gurney, *The Hittites* (Baltimore: Penguin Books, 1952), pp. 23–24; *Encyclopaedia Britannica*, 1968, vol. 11, p. 551.

11. Roux, *Ancient Iraq*, p. 219.

12. Roux, *Ancient Iraq*, p. 219; Starr, *Ancient World*, p. 102.

13. Gurney, *The Hittites*, pp. 23–24; Roux, *Ancient Iraq*, p. 219; Starr, *Ancient World*, p. 102; *Encyclopaedia Britannica*, 1968, vol. 2, p. 763.

14. Rather more than a thousand years later, King Cyrus II of Persia seems to have used one of these two openings in the city wall to enter Babylon and capture the city.

15. Roux, *Ancient Iraq*, p. 220, 221; *Encyclopaedia Britannica*, 1968, vol. 11, p. 551.

16. 'Gurney, *The Hittites*, p. 24; Roux, *Ancient Iraq*, pp. 221, 228.

17. Roux, *Ancient Iraq*, pp. 212, 230–31; Starr, *Ancient World*, pp. 85–86; Oppenheim, *Ancient Mesopotamia*, pp. 399–400.

18. Roux, *Ancient Iraq*, pp. 231, 233–34; Gurney, *The Hittites*, pp. 23, 28–30; Oppenheim, *Ancient Mesopotamia*, p. 400. Aleppo had been a not very docile vassal city-state under Hattusilis I. It was sacked by Mursilis I. During nearly all of the period from 1600 to 1450 B.C., the Hittites had been too weak to exert any significant influence in Syria, except that King Tudhaliyas (c. 1460–1440) may have sacked Aleppo.

19. Roux, *Ancient Iraq*, pp. 221 ff.

20. Gurney, *The Hittites*, pp. 26, 216.

21. Gurney, *The Hittites*, pp. 70, 105–6, 108–10, and plate 3; *Encyclopaedia Britannica*, 1929, vol. 22, p. 589; *Encyclopaedia Britannica*, 1968, vol. 2, p. 444.

22. Gurney, *The Hittites*, pp. 52, 86–87, 106, 109–10, 178–79.

23. Ibid., pp. 110–13.

24. Gurney, *The Hittites*, pp. 70–72, 80–92, 95–97; *Encyclopaedia Britannica*, 1929, vol. 2, pp. 865–66; vol. 11, p. 606; *Encyclopaedia Britannica*, 1968, vol. 11, p. 554. It is interesting that while this "code" prescribes various prices and rates of pay and prescribes the hiring rate for a plough ox, there appears to be no clause that prescribes an interest rate. Possibly in Anatolia as in Syria and Palestine there was a tabu on charging interest. Cf. Oppenheim, *Ancient Mesopotamia*, pp. 88–90.

25. Gurney, *The Hittites*, pp. 158, 173–77, 180, 197–98, 210.

26. Gurney, *The Hittites*, pp. 38–39, 216; *Encyclopaedia Britannica*, 1968, vol. 11, p. 554.

Section IV. The Phoenicians and Early Warships

As early as 2650 B.C., there was a seaworthy merchant vessel of the type known as a Byblos ship. These ships were presumably built at Byblos and built by Phoenician workmen. Certainly the lumber to build them came from Lebanon. Certainly, too, they were used for transporting cedar to Egypt during the period of the Old Kingdom (c. 2700 to 200 B.C.). We know that relations between Egypt and Byblos were friendly at this time and that the Egyptians had a trading post at Byblos. We do not know who owned the ships. It seems likely that they were owned in Byblos and manned by a Phoenician crew and that they visited other places on the Mediterranean as well as Egypt.[1]

The Egyptians also had a ship with a bifid mast that was used for transporting freight up and down the Nile. Quite possibly, too, they sometimes used a Byblos ship for this kind of traffic. If so, this Byblos ship was doubtless owned by Egypt.[2]

The Byblos ship had a single mast that supported a square sail. Besides the sail there were rowers; how many there were is not clear. This ship certainly was primarily a merchant vessel, but possibly it served at times as a pirate ship. In the third millenium B.C. and perhaps during a considerable part of the second, the distinction between a merchant and a combat vessel was pretty much a matter of the arms carried by the crew.[3]

Egypt was essentially a nonmoney economy during the third millenium B.C. so far as internal trading was concerned; that is, there was little if any internal trading. But agents of the king engaged in a good deal of external trading. Egypt had a large supply of trinkets and other articles made of gold, silver, copper, etc., that it could give in exchange for the lumber it needed. And quite possibly the Phoenicians supplied Egypt with other things beside lumber, perhaps olive oil and wine.[4]

We know little about the development of seagoing vessels during the third millennium B.C. either in Mesopotamia or in what is now Pakistan and western India. But it seems clear that there were somewhat extensive trade contacts across the

Indian Ocean c. 2000 B.C. There were shipyards in Sumer at this time in which quite large seagoing vessels were built, probably for carrying the merchandise these contacts involved. And at a place not far from modern Bombay there are the remains of a dockyard some seven hundred feet long. This was probably built early in the second millennium B.C.[5]

It seems clear that there were merchant ships, particularly freighters, long before there were any seagoing vessels that could properly be called men-of war. We know that before the middle of the fifteenth century B.C., the Egyptians had a boat that was able to bring two great obelisks down the Nile from Aswan to Karnak for Queen Hat-shepsut (c. 1486 to 1468). Each obelisk must have weighed more than thirty-five tons. The boat was a barge that was towed by thirty rowboats, each of which had thirty oarsmen.[6]

The first warship we have any information about probably dates something like two centuries before the end of the second millennium B.C. It was a Greek galley with twenty-five oarsmen on each side that was called a Penteconter. It was presumably commanded as well as steered by the man who managed the stern sweep. It had two masts that carried sails. It must have been at least ninety feet long. It was an open boat without any deck. The rowers apparently sat on thwarts which served as cross-braces for the hull. Some of these ships had rams projecting from their bows. Penteconters were said to have been used in the Trojan war. It seems likely that they were sometimes used for piracy.[7]

There must have been a period following the development of this man-of-war during which there was pressure toward building swifter and more powerful warships. Apparently it did not seem advisable greatly to increase the length of a ship. Such an increase would decrease its maneuverability and aggravate the problem of constructing a ship that could not hog or sag in the middle. The result of this situation was that a bireme was invented, a galley with two tiers of oarsmen. It seems probable that this invention took place early in the first millennium B.C. and that the Phoenicians are to be credited with it. At all events, our principal source of information about biremes is pictures of Phoenician galleys on the walls of an Assyrian palace that must have been painted during the eighth century B.C. Each ship was armed with a ram that had a metal head or beak. The ram projected from the bow. The ship was aphract, that is, the rowers in the upper tier were out in the open.[8]

Triremes apparently superseded biremes about the middle of the first millennium B.C. On the Greek trireme the ram seems to have projected from the stern just above the waterline. The beak was made of hard bronze. Somewhat higher up, there was a second ram, the end of which was also made of hard bronze. This one was shorter. Its purpose was thought to be to help in disentangling the ship from a rammed enemy vessel that was sinking. Probably at the time of the battle of Salamis (480 B.C.), each trireme in the Greek navy was strengthened by heavy rope girdles, usually two or more, that passed all of the way around the ship above the waterline. Each girdle was put on tightly, and then, when it shrank, it became tighter still. A main purpose of these girdles was to enable the ship to withstand the shock of ramming an enemy vessel. Each Greek trireme also had a kind of wooden armor plate, that is, a second layer of wood that was carried from stem to stern around the vessel as a protection against enemy rams. The ship was steered by two rudders operated with tillers, one rudder on either side of the ship at its stern.[9]

The crew of a Greek trireme at this time probably consisted of two hundred odd men. There were perhaps 170 or more oarsmen and thirty or more seamen and marines. The ship was captained by a trierarch. The second in command was the helmsman.[10]

The Phoenician ships that fought in the battle of Salamis were probably quite similar to the Greek triremes. Presumably either the Greeks had copied the Phoenician design for triremes, or the Phoenicians had taken their design from the Greeks; we do not know which. However, there were some differences. The Phoenician ships were lighter and faster. They

97

were designed primarily for boarding tactics; the Greek ships were designed more especially for ramming. And since the Phoenician ships were fighting for Persia, their marines were Persians, and there were more marines.[11] One implement used in naval warfare that may well have been developed by the time of the battle of Salamis is the grappling iron. It was used by both the Athenians and the Syracusans in sea fighting at Syracuse during the Peloponnesian war.[12]

The rest of this section goes somewhat beyond the general subject, "Developments in Military Technology and Government Organization in the Ancient Near East." It includes comments on warships during and somewhat after the fourth century B.C. and on Phoenician economic history.

The trireme was superseded by the quadrireme and the quinquereme. Then there seems to have been a type of galley called the hexeris. And in the battle of Salamis (off Cyprus) in 306 B.C., Demetrius I had a fleet of hepteres with which he defeated the fleet of Ptolemy I. The hepteris was apparently a ship with a single bank of oars and seven men to each oar. The hexeris was presumably a ship with six men per oar. In the third century there were galleys with two or more banks of oars and several men to each oar. Antigonas Gonatas had a galley referred to as an eighteen, probably a trireme with six men to each oar. It was his flagship in a battle off Cos c. 257 B.C., in which he defeated Ptolemy II. After that, there were at least experiments with still more powerful warships. Ptolemy IV is said to have built a forty, a quadrireme with ten men per oar, that did not prove to be successful.[13]

During the First Punic War, the Carthaginians relied extensively on quinqueremes, and the Romans presently adopted the Carthaginian model. Each oar was apparently manned by a crew of five. About 260 B.C., the Romans developed what they called a *corvus,* which was a bridge that could be lowered onto an enemy ship when their ship had come alongside it. With the *corvus* they were able to put a large boarding party on board an enemy ship. This was such a successful combat device

98

that they soon dominated the Mediterranean. But it made their ships top-heavy. Partly because of this, partly because the Romans had had little experience with rough weather, about 255 B.C., they suffered a series of naval disasters in which they lost over five hundred warships and perhaps one thousand transports.[14]

In 31 B.C., in the battle of Actium, Octavian had a flotilla of swift, easy-to-manage biremes of a new design called Liburnians that, under Agrippa, outmaneuvered and defeated Antony's quinqueremes and burned many of them. Thereafter, quinqueremes seem to have been relatively unimportant. And in the fifth century A.D. biremes were superseded by a speedy type of fighting vessels called Dromons that had a single tier of oarsmen.[15]

During most of the period with which this essay is concerned, c. 2700 to 324 B.C., Phoenician city-states were considered by the dominant power of the day, from Babylonia under Hammurabi to Alexander the Great, to be more or less under the empire's dominion. However, during the Old Kingdom in Egypt, Byblos was an independent city-state, quite possibly the most prosperous and most important of the little kingdoms into which Phoenicia was divided. During the latter half of the second millennium B.C., Ugarit became a major manufacturing and trading center and the wealthiest of the Phoenician city-states. She produced an extensive literature written in an alphabetic cuneiform script. Ugarit, like the Hittite Empire, was overrun and destroyed by a horde of sea people from the north c. 1200 B.C.[16]

Other Phoenician cities that had been overrun recovered fairly promptly. Sidon, Tyre, Byblos and Aradus (or Arvad) became very prosperous, particularly Tyre. By the tenth century B.C., Tyre had become a great trading and manufacturing port, probably the leading commercial and manufacturing center of the day. During the next hundred odd years, she founded a number of colonies, among them Carthage. C. 887, and again c. 840 B.C., perhaps also on other occasions, she was compelled to pay tribute to Assyria. But the Assyrians liked to hire

Phoenician seamen and Phoenician ships, as did the Persians in a later period. Hence, during the Assyrian Empire and also during the Persian Empire, Phoenician city-states enjoyed a good deal of freedom. But Tyre's mercantile and industrial pre-eminence made her a military target. She was besieged by Nebuchadrezzar from 585 to 573 B.C. and by Alexander the Great some 250 years later. We shall consider each of these sieges in a subsequent chapter.[17]

The Phoenicians had colonies and trading posts in various places, several of them on Cyprus, Utica and Carthage in Africa, Gadir (or Gadeira, modern Cadiz) in what is now Spain, and a number of others. To handle the imports from and exports to these colonies and outposts, they must have had a large and efficient merchant fleet. We have little information about the number of ships they had or about what their ships were like. The Bible tells us that Hiram, King of Tyre, provided Solomon, King of Israel and Judah, with a fleet that sailed from Exiongeber at the head of the Gulf of Aqaba to a place called Ophir and brought back gold as well as lumber that was used to make pillars for the temple Solomon was building. This expedition took place about 950 B.C. We can be sure the ships were quite small. During the early sixth century, sailing vessels were still small enough to be dragged over the four-mile span of the Isthmus of Corinth on a slideway, or diolkos, the Corinthians had built to facilitate the portaging.

But even before 600 B.C. Phoenician ships were venturing out into the Atlantic. They were undoubtedly square-rigged sailing vessels; each ship presumably had at least one pair of oars for maneuvering in a harbor. The Phoenicians were skilled navigators, the first people to use the North Star to steer by. They apparently knew a great deal about tides, currents, and prevailing winds, about harbors in various places and the entrances to them, about rocks and shoals that were to be avoided. They regarded what they knew about these things as trade secrets. They must have had records of what they knew; but whether they had charts seems doubtful.[18]

The Phoenicians were skilled metal workers, makers of

textiles, and makers of glassware. They were famed for their purple dye; the Tyrians had a secret process for making it. As merchants they had to make a great many arithmetical computations. Apparently they invented an abacus. They passed on to the Greeks, among other things, their alphabet and their system of weights and measures.[19]

Notes

Section IV.

1. R. W. Hutchinson, *Prehistoric Crete* (Baltimore: Penguin Books, 1962); John A. Wilson, *The Culture of Ancient Egypt* (Chicago: University of Chicago Press, 1951), pp. 82, 100–1; *Encyclopaedia Britannica,* 1968, vol. 8, pp. 34, 46; vol. 17, pp. 886, 890. There were apparently some forty Byblos ships operating in the twenty-sixth century B.C.
2. Hutchinson, *Prehistoric Crete,* p. 93.
3. Ibid.
4. Wilson, *Ancient Egypt,* pp. 82–83, 100–1.
5. Bridget and Raymond Allchin, *The Birth of Indian Civilization* (Baltimore: Penguin Books, 1968), pp. 131, 141, 240–41, 271, 322; Georges Roux, *Ancient Iraq* (Harmondsworth, Middlesex, England: Penguin Books, 1966; first published by George Allen & Unwin, 1964), p. 148; Chester G. Starr, *A History of the Ancient World* (New York: Oxford University Press, 1965), p. 113; *Encyclopaedia Britannica,* 1968, vol. 12, p. 188.
6. Hutchinson, *Prehistoric Crete,* p. 99; *Encyclopaedia Britannica,* 1929, vol. 10, p. 667; *Encyclopaedia Britannica,* 1968, vol. 8, p. 47.
7. Xenophon, *Anabasis,* rev. ed., edited and with an introduction by William W. Goodwin and John Williams White; Greek-English dictionary by John Williams White and Morris H. Morgan (New York: Ginn & Co., 1894), p. 174 of the dictionary; *Encyclopaedia Britannica,* 1968, vol. 20, p. 399.
8. *Encyclopaedia Britannica,* 1929, vol. 20, p. 506; *Encyclopaedia Britannica,* 1968, vol. 17, pp. 890–91; vol. 20, p. 399.
9. *Encyclopaedia Britannica,* 1929, vol. 20, pp. 506–7; *Encyclopaedia Britannica,* 1968, vol. 10, p. 798; vol. 20, p. 400.
10. *Encyclopaedia Britannica,* 1929, vol. 20, p. 507; Xenophon, *Anabasis,* dictionary p. 221. According to this dictionary, the helmsman was captain, and the second officer was stationed at the bow.
11. *Encyclopaedia Britannica,* 1968, vol. 10, p. 798; vol. 17, p. 660.
12. Thucidides, *Peloponnesian War,* trans. Richard Crawley (London: J. M. Dent and Sons, Ltd., 1910), pp. 262, 520, 522.
13. W. W. Tarn, *Hellenistic Civilization* (New York: World Publishing Company, 1952), pp. 58–59; *Encyclopaedia Britannica,* 1929, vol. 18; *Encyclopaedia Britannica,* 1968, vol. 20 p. 399;
14. Starr, *Ancient World,* p. 481; Pierre Grimal, *Hellenism and the Rise*

of Rome (New York: Delacorte Press, 1965), pp. 309–10; *Encyclopaedia Britannica,* 1929, vol. 1, p. 140; vol. 20, p. 507.

15. Starr, *Ancient World,* p. 551; *Encyclopaedia Britannica,* 1929, vol. 1, p. 140, vol. 20, p. 507.

16. Roux, *Ancient Iraq,* pp. 215, 232, 234, 243, 321; Cyrus H. Gordon, *The Ancient Near East* (New York: W. W. Norton & Co., 1965; originally published as *The World of the Old Testament,* Ventnor Publishers, 1953), chap. VI; *Encyclopaedia Britannica,* 1968, vol. 22, p. 466.

17. Roux, *Ancient Iraq,* pp. 243, 262, 269; Gordon, *The Ancient Near East,* pp. 186–87, 262–63, 288; *Encyclopaedia Britannica,* 1929, vol. 17, p. 769; *Encyclopaedia Britannica,* 1968, vol. 4, p. 976; vol. 22, p. 452.

18. Bible (King James Version), I Kings 9: 26–28, 10: 11, 12, 22; Starr, *Ancient World,* p. 128; Gordon, *The Ancient Near East,* p. 187; *Encyclopaedia Britannica,* 1929, vol. 17, p. 769; *Encyclopaedia Britannica,* 1968, vol. 10, p. 794; vol. 17, pp. 606, 887–90. The location of Ophir has not been determined. The diolkos was probably built about 600 B.C. by Periander, who was then tyrant of Corinth. Of course, sailors had long been using the stars to sail by; the use of Polaris by the Phoenicians meant a more precise type of observation.

19. Starr, *Ancient World,* pp. 127–28; R. J. Forbes, "Chemical, Culinary, and Cosmetic Arts," in *A History of Technology,* eds. Charles Singer, E. J. Holmyard, and A. R. Hall (New York: Oxford University Press, 1954), vol. 1, pp. 247–48; *Encyclopaedia Britannica,* 1968, vol. 17, pp. 886–93.

Section V. The Assyrian Empire

Early in the second millenium BC., Assur became a city-state to be reckoned with, but the Assyrian kingdom continued to be small for more than a thousand years. It began to expand under Adad-nirari II (c. 911 to 891 B.C.), and both his grandson, Ashurnasirpal II (c. 833 to 859 B. C.), and his great grandson, Shalmaneser III (c. 858 to 824 B.C.), made extensive additions to Assyrian territory.[1]

The greatness of the Assyrian Empire was to a considerable extent due to the outstanding superiority of its military establishment. This superiority was partly a matter of new technology it was quick to adopt, partly a matter of its size and efficient organization.

One new feature of the Assyrian army was its cavalry division; the Assyrians were apparently the first to have such a unit. Apparently, the cavalryman rode his horse with just a saddle cloth. Saddles and stirrups were much later developments. Little is known about the size of the Assyrian cavalry force; but there must have been a substantial number of cavalrymen, for there were several grades of cavalry officers. Each mounted man was armed either with a small bow and arrows or with a long spear. At least during the latter part of the seventh century B.C., both horse and rider wore protective armor.[2]

The army included a chariot force that was doubtless modeled on that of the Hyksos and that of the Hittites. The chariots were a little heavier. Some of them were drawn by a three-horse team. The crew consisted of three or four men, the driver and one or two bowmen and shieldbearers. Not much is known about the tactics of the Assyrian army; but it seems clear that with its cavalry division and its chariot force, it was well equipped to ravage the countryside. The extensive military operations of both Ashurnasirpal II and his son, Shalmaneser, seem to have consisted in considerable part of raids on unfortified towns and villages.[3]

The army included a substantial number of both light and

heavily armed infantrymen. The former were mostly slingers. Apparently they usually fought bareheaded. The latter were armed either with bows and arrows or with lances. They wore helmets and coats of mail and carried shields some of which were taller than the soldiers. Presumably they fought in a phalanx formation. Most infantrymen of both types were armed with short swords, daggers, or maces. One of the advantages the Assyrian army had was that the various weapons, spears, lances, swords, etc., were made of iron. It was apparently the first major army to be so equipped.[4]

We have few reports on the size of the Assyrian army. Shalmaneser III claims that in the battle of Qarqar (c. 853 B.C.) he had a force of 120,000 men; and his father, Ashurnasirpal II, in reporting an action some years earlier, refers to a force of 50,000. We have no way of knowing how much exaggeration these figures may involve; they seem quite large. In any case, the army was doubtless adequately financed and supplied so that it could carry out a prolonged, long-distance operation and could maintain a siege. Tiglath Pileser III besieged Arpad, the capital of a small city-state in Syria, for three years; it finally succumbed in 741 B.C. Simply listing the places in which the army operated makes it clear that it was skillfully managed and that it was a very mobile force able to traverse various types of difficult territory. It conducted campaigns in Tabal, Cilicia, and Kurdistan in Asia Minor, around Lake Van and Lake Urmiah in northern Iraq, on the Iranian plateau, in the Arabian desert, in Phoenicia, Palestine, and Egypt, and along the Persian Gulf and in Elam.[5]

What has been said about the Assyrian cavalry, chariot force, and infantry, and about the size, management, and mobility of the army goes a long way toward explaining its outstanding superiority. But something needs to be said, also, about the army's noncombat units, the engineer corps and the beginnings of a quartermaster corps. It is probable that the engineer corps was extremely well equpped even before the middle of the ninth century B.C. In his annals Ashurnasirpal II records taking a strongly fortified city in northern Syria he calls Kaprabi with the aid of "mines, battering-rams and siege engines." The engines were probably catapults, machines that fired stones, arrows, and other projectiles at enemy targets. There is some reason to believe that the Assyrians had developed them as early as the thirteenth century B.C. The propulsion mechanism of a catapult consisted of a skein of elastic materials, sinew, hair, or rope, that was suspended vertically between an upper and a lower sill, and a bar that was inserted in the skein and rotated so as to wind the skein up very tight; when unwinding was suddenly permitted the missile was propelled forward with considerable speed. In Ashurnasirpal's day, the propulsion mechanism probably consisted of two skeins, the unwinding of which could be simultaneously released.[6]

By the time of Tiglath Pileser III (c. 745–27 B.C.), probably even somewhat before that, the Assyrian engineer corps was equipped to fill moats, dig tunnels, and build roads and earthworks. The engineers built and moved mobile towers from which catapults could be operated and from which bowmen could shoot their arrows. They had small boats; they set up pontoon bridges for crossing streams. They operated heavy battering-rams that were mounted on wheels. Their siege equipment included ladders, also testudines or rats, large shields used to protect men engaged in undermining a city wall against rocks or burning oil thrown from above by the city's defenders.[7]

Cyrus H. Gordon, discussing developments during the reign of Tiglath Pileser III, says "The Assyrian regime . . . developed siege warfare to a greater extent than ever before; battering-rams and other devices for breaching strong city walls." Gordon does not indicate the nature of these developments; but we know something about the steps by which battering-rams developed, and it is reasonable to suppose one or more of these steps to have been taken about 740 or 730 B.C. Others were doubtless taken before that. Originally a battering-ram was just a very heavy pole wielded by a crew of no more than a dozen men. From time to time its size and weight were increased and the size of the crew was increased accordingly. It is said that eventually, possibly some time A.D., a crew of more than two hundred men was used. Perhaps quite early the business end of the ram was protected by a metal cap, presumably bronze at first, probably by 740 B.C. by an iron cap. As the weight of the ram was increased, it was presently discovered, possibly during the time with which we are here concerned, that the ram could be wielded much more effectively if it were suspended from an overhead beam. Sometimes this beam was a part of the testudo structure in which the ram was housed.[8]

Whatever improvements in siege equipment were made during the reign of Tiglath Pileser seem to have facilitated taking walled cities. In his annals, Sennacherib claims that during a campaign in Palestine in 701 B.C., he took forty-six walled cities. Apparently at this time only Jerusalem was able to stand out against him.[9]

It is not clear how much the Assyrian army had in the way of a quartermaster corps. Certainly it included a wagon train for the transportation of baggage, supplies, and equipment. One expedition obviously involved a substantial transportation problem. Sennacherib, c. 695 B.C., took his army down the Tigris and Euphrates rivers to the Persian Gulf and then north into Elam. The expedition went down the Tigris to a place he calls Upā in a fleet of boats that had been constructed for the purpose and that was manned by Phoenician and Cypriot seamen. From Upā the army and the ships were transported overland westward to a canal and then to the Euphrates. The expedition next proceeded down the Euphrates to the Gulf, then overland again into Elam.[10]

The army's incipient quartermaster corps must have been a good deal more than a transport service. It presumably had responsibilities in connection with the making and breaking up of camps. And at least by the time of Ashurnasirpal II, the army had become too big to provide food for itself by foraging. Perhaps it operated a mess service. But it seems more likely that at each major camp it set up a canteen at which the soldiers could buy food and drinks. This kind of service could hardly have been adequately provided for by the troupe of men and women camp followers that the army doubtless called into being.[11]

Tiglath Pileser III ascended the throne of Assyria c. 745 B.C. For nearly forty years before that the empire had had a series of three rather ineffective rulers, Tiglath Pileser's brothers. He began his reign with a successful military campaign in Syria, a reform of civil administration, and a reorganization of the army, making it for the first time a standing army. The changes in civil administration he effected were particularly important. Assyria proper (the area of the Kingdom c. 900 B.C.) had consisted of several cities, each of which had a separate government and a number of rural districts ruled by lords who had enjoyed a good deal of independence. The local city councils apparently continued to have a fair amount to say about local affairs after his administrative reform. He made the rural districts smaller and more numerous to reduce the powers of the lords and make them more responsible to the crown. Various countries that had been conquered and had become parts of the empire were made provinces. He appointed a governor—usually an Assyrian—to govern each province. He established an efficient messenger service to carry reports and letters from the rural district lords and province governors to the king and orders to them issued by the king. There were special runners that carried communications requiring prompt delivery. Also, he established an inspector system to check on the operatons of the rural lords and province governors. In addition to Assyria proper and the provinces, the empire included various territories that merely paid tribute to avoid harassing raids.[12]

The army as reorganized by Tiglath Pileser was mainly provided by quotas levied on the provinces. These quotas not only replaced conscripts from Assyria proper, but they also made possible a substantial increase in the size of the army. Also it was now a standing army. In addition to the quotas, the army included mercenaries, and there were various fortresses garrisoned by Assyrians. No doubt, too, most army officers continued to be Assyrians, and the royal guard continued to consist of Assyrians.[13]

Another change initiated by Tiglath Pileser relates to the treatment of the conquered peoples. He started a practice of mass deportation. Thousands of people were evicted from their native habitats and compelled to settle in distant parts of the empire. The theory that was the basis for this practice seems to have been that it would prevent the loyalty of a people to their local gods and traditions from hampering the development of a proper respect for the Assyrian empire and its interests. This practice was added to other cruel practices begun by Tiglath Pileser's predecessors, notably by Ashurnasirpal II, large-scale massacres of captives taken in battle, and large-scale mutilations of various parts of the bodies of captives that were allowed to live. There was also a practice of displaying prominently the heads and skulls of local rulers and numerous others that had been decapitated. These practices were doubtless intended to instill an attitude of obedience to the king and to discourage insurrections. One result of all these practices was that the Assyrians were widely hated. Whatever else they accomplished, they did not prevent insurrections. The empire army had repeatedly to act to put them down.[14]

Assyrians were concerned with other matters beside waging wars, maintaining empire discipline, and governing efficiently. For our present purpose, we shall comment only on their construction activies and on developments that accompanied them. The Assyrians were great builders of temples, palaces, and city walls. Let us characterize briefly the empire's three largest construction undertakings: (1) Probably between 717 and 708 B.C., Sargon II had a new capital built at a place he called Dur-Sharrukīn. It was about fifteen miles from Nineveh. This project included a seven-story ziggurat, a fortress, and a sumptuous palace. (2) During the reign of Sennacherib (c. 704 to 681 B.C.) Nineveh was enlarged and provided with a magnificent palace. The city was encircled by a great double wall and an outside moat. The wall was about eight miles long.

There was an aqueduct to bring fresh water into the city. (3) Esarhaddon, during his reign (c. 680 to 669 B.C.), rebuilt, enlarged, and embellished Babylon—it had been sacked by Sennacherib as punishment for rebelling in 689 B.C. On each of these three undertakings, tens of thousands of man-years must have been employed.[15]

In addition to palaces, temples, and city walls, the Assyrians did a great deal of construction work on roads and irrigation systems. As a result of what they did for irrigation, there was a substantial increase in the area of farm land under intensive cultivation. Partly as a consequence of this and as a response to the stimulus of their construction activities, partly as an accompaniment of the Pax Assyriana that they more or less successfully maintained for a hundred and thirty-odd years, there was a considerable increase in production and in intercommunity trade and a concommitant increase in population.[16]

In 1750 B.C., the Assyrians had not been greatly influenced by the developments in technology and buisness and industry in lower Mesopotamia. By 744 B.C., they had largely taken over Babylonian culture. They doubtless admired, and perhaps looked up to, the people from whom they had borrowed so much. At least one great Assyrian monarch seems to have been anxious to demonstrate that he was quite as learned as the Babylonians, Ashurbanipal (c. 668 to 627 B.C.) He built up a very extensive library that included both letters, contracts, and other archive documents and literary, religious, and scientific compositions. While most of the Assyrian labor force was undoubtedly engaged in agriculture and animal husbandry, there were also many highly skilled handicraftsmen. Some of them were non-Assyrian employees; some of them were captive slaves. Assyria had become a money economy with silver as a standard of value and with people engaged in lending and borrowing transactions. Trade routes connected the various parts of the empire. Assyrian might reflected the technology and warfare methods they had borrowed and improved upon. But the Assyrians had borrowed not only from lower Mesopotamia; they had borrowed also from other neighboring peoples. From the Hyksos and the Hittites they got their light chariots. Also from the Hittites, they borrowed the practice of decorating palace walls with bas-relief pictures and the kingly custom of writing annals of royal achievements, to which we are indebted for much of what we know about Assyrian history.[17]

The empire came to an end c. 612 B.C.

Notes

Section V.

1. Georges Roux, *Ancient Iraq* (Harmondsworth, Middlesex, England: Penguin Books, 1966; first published by George Allen & Unwin, 1964), chap. 18, pp. 173–75; *Encyclopaedia Britannica*, 1929, vol. 2, p. 849.

2. Roux, *Ancient Iraq*, p. 316; A. Leo Oppenheim, *Ancient Mesopotamia: Portrait of a Dead Civilization* (Chicago: University of Chicago Press, 1964), pp. 46, 166.

3. Roux, *Ancient Iraq*, p. 316; Chester G. Starr, *A History of the Ancient World* (New York: Oxford University Press, 1965), p.132.

4. Roux, *Ancient Iraq*, p. 316; Starr, *Ancient World*, p. 32. It is quite possible that the Hittites had some iron weapons. See *Encyclopedia Britannica*, 1968, vol. 21, p. 604.

5. Roux, *Ancient Iraq*, pp. 274–75, 279, 282–84, 289, 291, 297–98, 302, 315; Starr, *Ancient World*, p. 133. Shalmaneser's figure of 120,000 men may be compared with the figure of 150,000 that Chester G. Starr suggests for the great army of Xerxes I with which he started out in 481 B.C. to overrun Greece. Arpad was not far from Aleppo.

6. Roux, *Ancient Iraq*, p. 262; *Encyclopaedia Britannica*, 1968, vol. 21, p. 604; Major General J. F. C. Fuller, *The Generalship of Alexander the Great* (New York: Funk and Wagnalls, paperback edition 1968, published by arrangement with Rutgers University Press, copyright 1960), pp. 44, 45; *Encyclopaedia Britannica*, 1929, vol. 2, p. 851. *Encyclopaedia Britannica*, 1968, vol. 8, pp. 399–400; vol. 21, p. 604. Georges Roux thinks Kaprabi may have been Urfa, Syria. In the eighth century B.C., catapults seem to have been widely used. In Judah, King Uzziah (c. 808 to 756 B. C.; his name is also written Azariah) had them. See the Bible (King James Version), II Chronicles 26: 15; *Encyclopaedia Britannica* 1929, vol. 8, p. 453.

7. Roux, *Ancient Iraq*, pp. 316–17; *Encyclopaedia Britannica*, 1929, vol. 2, p. 851.

8. Cyrus H. Gordon, *The Ancient Near East* (New York: W. W. Norton & Co., 1965; originally published as *The World of the Old Testament*, Ventnor

110

Publishers, 1953), 227–28; *Encyclopaedia Britannica*, 1968, vol. 8, p. 400; vol. 21, p. 604.

9. Gordon, *The Ancient Near East*, p. 237.

10. Roux, *Ancient Iraq*, pp. 290–91, 316. The location of Upā is not known; Seleucia may have been built on the site of Upā. See Roux, *Ancient Iraq*, p. 378.

11. Fuller, *Alexander the Great*, p. 53, says: "An army of between 30,000 and 50,000 men, without counting followers, can seldom be adequately supplied by foraging."

12. Roux, *Ancient Iraq*, pp. 276–77, 310, 313; Starr, *Ancient World*, pp. 131–32; *Encyclopaedia Britannica*, 1968, vol. 21, p. 1143.

13. Roux, *Ancient Iraq*, pp. 277–78; Starr, *Ancient World*, p. 132; *Encyclopaedia Britannica*, 1929, vol. 2, pp. 850–51.

14. Roux, *Ancient Iraq*, pp. 262–63, 278, 280–85, 278–89, 295, 299–303; Oppenheim, *Ancient Mesopotamia*, pp. 119, 169; Gordon, *The Ancient Near East*, p. 227.

15. Roux, *Ancient Iraq*, pp. 264–67, 280, 285–86, 291–92, 294; Gordon, *The Ancient Near East*, pp. 232, 235–36, 252; Oppenheim, *Ancient Mesopotamia*, pp. 94, 108, 140.

16. Starr, *Ancient World*, p. 134. See also M. J. Drower, "Water-supply, Irrigation, and Agriculture," in *A History of Technology*, eds. Charles Singer, E. J. Holmyard, and A. R. Hall (New York: Oxford University Press, 1954), vol. 1, pp. 531–34; S. M. Cole, "Roads," in *A History of Technology*, eds. Charles Singer, E. J. Holmyard, and A. R. Hall (New York:Oxford University Press, 1954), vol. 1, p. 714.

17. Roux, *Ancient Iraq*, pp. 318, 323–34; Gurney, *The Hittites* (Baltimore: Penguin Books, 1952), pp. 177, 210; Starr, *Ancient World* pp. 134–36.

Section VI. Nebuchadrezzar and the Persians

The Assyrian Empire collapsed not long after the death of Ashurbanipal c. 627 B.C. It had depended for empire unity on having loyal Assyrians in key positions. But various important officials appear to have had a thirty-year tenure. And with the growth in size of officialdom and the increase in the wealth and luxury at its disposal, self-seeking and palace intrigue seem presently to have to some extent replaced loyalty to the king. The situation may be said to have been ripe for a rapid disintegration of the empire.[1]

Nabopolassar, c. 626 B.C., an Aramaean, a member of a tribe called Kaldū, seized power in Babylon and founded what is known as the Chaldaean or Neo-Babylonian dynasty. During the next ten or eleven years, he campaigned against Assyria to take over all of lower Mesopotamia. Media, an Indo-European kingdom in northwestern Iran, sent an invasionary force into Assyria and captured Assur, c. 615 B.C. The Medes and the Babylonians became allies. Nabopolassar's son, Nebuchadrezzar, married the daughter of King Cyaxares of Media. The fate of Assyria was sealed. Probably by the end of 612 B.C. the Medes and the Babylonians between them had taken all three Assyrian capital cities, Assur, the religious center, Nimrud, the army headquarters, and Nineveh.[2]

Not much is known about the military establishment of the Medes. In view of its success against Assyria, it must have been both powerful and thoroughly up-to-date. Except for a part of Syria, the Medes do not seem to have been interested in holding territory in the Fertile Crescent. When they and the Babylonians divided up the former Assyrian empire, the Medes took northern Syria, Armenia, the part of the former empire to the north and east of the Zagros mountains, and Elam. The Babylonians took Mesopotamia and fought, eventually successfully, for the rest of Syria and Palestine.[3]

Nebuchadrezzar's military activities were concerned largely with this area. While still crown prince, he succeeded, during 607–605 B.C., in taking it over from Egypt. But thereafter he had repeatedly to put down rebellions of Phoenicians, Philistines, and Judeans. Jerusalem revolted in 597 B.C. and again eight years later. There were extensive deportations after the earlier revolt, still more extensive deportations after the second one. Jerusalem was taken in 587 B.C. after an eighteen-month siege, and the great temple was destroyed. Beginning in 585 B.C., Nebuchadrezzar besieged Tyre. This siege lasted eleven years. Nebuchadrezzar's army never entered the island city, but a new king was put on its throne in 573 B.C., and Tyre became a part of the Neo-Babylonian empire.[4]

Nebuchadrezzar was particularly proud of his building activites. These included major reconstruction projects in a number of Mesopotamian cities, notably in Babylon. The great new city wall was thirty-six feet wide at its top and perhaps thirty feet high. Near the great Ishtar gate, he built a huge palace. This probably included the "hanging gardens" that became one of the seven wonders of antiquity. He rebuilt the mammoth ziggurat—the "tower of Babel"—and the temple of Marduk. Nebuchadrezzar's construction activites also included extensive improvements in the country's irrigation system.[5]

If the Neo-Babylonian dynasty was responsible for any significant improvements either in military technology or in government organization, it is not possible today to specify them. However, it was characterized by a religious revival and something of a renaissance. But the dynasty was decidedly short-lived. It came to an end in 539 B.C. when Babylon was taken without resistance by Cyrus II. None-the-less, intellectual activity seems to have continued on at least one front. During the two hundred years that followed the collapse of the Neo-Babylonian empire, Babylonian astronomers made records of the observed positions of the sun, moon, and planets. On the basis of these records they developed predictions of eclipses and other astronomic events.[6]

Cyrus II inherited a small kingdom, Persia, from his father, Cambyses I. According to Herodotus, Mandane, the wife of Cambyses and mother of Cyrus, was a daughter of Astyages, king of Media. At all events, c. 550 B.C. there was a war between the Medes and the Persians, between Astyages and Cyrus. Cyrus won and became king of both states. Not long after that, he set out on a series of campaigns. In 547 B.C., he defeated Croesus and thus conquered the wealthy country of Lydia. Next he conquered the Greek cities of Ionia, one after another. Then he pushed eastward through Turkestan and Afghanistan and into India. After he took Babylon in 539 B.C., Sumer and Akkad readily became parts of his empire. Much of his success in building up this great empire was due to his policy—very different from that of the Assyrians and Neo-Babylonians—of courting goodwill in the lands he took over. He posed as a liberator, returning displaced people to their former homes; he was merciful to prisoners; he respected the local customs and religions of his new subjects. In Babylon, he worshipped Marduk. His reign came to an untimely end in 530 B.C. He was killed in a battle against nomadic hill people in India.[7]

Only one major addition to the territory included in the Empire was made after he died. In 525 B.C., his son, Cambyses II, took Egypt. Continuing the policy of his father like a true Chaldean king, he "took the hand of Bel" (i.e., of Marduk) in the new year's festival at Babylon, and, in Egypt, he became a pharaoh. This policy may have been successful for a time. But in 522 B.C., a man called Bardiya revolted and seized the throne. Cambyses was wounded, probably in fighting him; he died in March 521.[8]

Darius I, a member of the royal family, fought and killed Bardiya. In 520 B.C., he became king, but during the first two or three years of his reign, he had several rebellions to put down. As soon as he was firmly established on the throne, he devoted himself to improving the organization of the Empire. Taking a cue from Tiglath Pileser, he increased the number of satrapies into which the Empire was divided and made them smaller. Each satrap ruled a semi-independent kingdom; he was a kind of vassal of the king. He had a military force of his own, but there was also an Empire army. He controlled the collection of taxes, turning over to the Empire treasury an amount dictated by the king. He could coin money, minor silver coins; only the king coined gold darics. He was expected to seek the counsel of the principal Persians living in his satrapy. The king had an Empire inspection service. The king controlled the Empire postal messenger service. It operated over a system of roads, the sixteen-hundred-mile royal road from Sardis to Susa and its various branches. There were rest houses along the roads, one hundred and eleven of them along the royal road. At each rest house guards were posted. There were mounted couriers on duty day and night. The roads were not what we should consider well paved; for much of the mileage, they were mere trails. But it is said that couriers could travel between Susa and Babylon at the rate of one hundred miles per day. Extensions of the royal road went to India; one trail went to Attock, a place on the upper Indus River just east of Peshawar.[9]

The Persians do not appear to have made important contributions to military technology or the methods of warfare. Cyrus relied heavily on his cavalry. His cavalrymen were mostly, perhaps entirely, wealthy Persians. Persumably, they owned their horses and equipment. At the battle of Cunaxa, c. 401 B.C., each cavalryman wore a helmet, a cuirass, and thigh armor, and the head and body of his horse were protected by armor. He carried a sword and two spears. The cavalry force that Cyrus took with him on his expeditions to India a hundred-odd years earlier may have been similarly equipped. What forces other than cavalry Cyrus took with him on these two expeditions we do not know, some infantry surely and engineers to provide siege equipment. Nor do we have any indication of the size of his cavalry force. But his army, though probably not very large, must have been large enough to require an efficient quartermaster service to provide food and other necessities, including transportation. As a tactician, Cyrus has been described as tricky. He put camels out in front of his fighting force to upset the horses of his enemy. He was apparently able to enter Babylon via the Euphrates River by going by boat along the canalized section of the river through the city to a suitable point and simply climbing over the levee. There seems to have been only a single small gate he had to break through; and the city was celebrating a feast day at the time.[10]

In the battle of Cunaxa, perhaps even before that, the Persians had a new type of chariot. It had scythes mounted on the hubs of the two wheels, and a long spear-headed pole that projected way out in front. Xenophon thought that the scythes and the spear-headed pole added little to the chariot's effectiveness, but Darius III had chariots of this type when he faced Alexander the Great at Arbela. He also had another new kind of military equipment: he had fifteen elephants. Just when the Persians took over the idea of using elephants from India is not clear, but, apparently, they were a better means of upsetting the enemy's horses than camels.[11]

Although there is no reason to suppose that the Persians ever used it, it may be appropriate to mention at this point an interesting type of siege equipment employed by the Peloponnesians in the Peloponnesian War. In the siege of Delium, they had a huge blowtorch. It was made by scooping "out a great beam from end to end, and fitting it nicely together again like a pipe" and plating the inside with iron. With this torch and a huge bellows, the besiegers were able to blow "lighted coals, sulphur, and pitch" onto the wooden fortifications of Delium and set fire to them.[12]

Between 499 and 449 B.C., the Persians and Greeks were engaged in a great war. Since the details of this war are not pertinent to our present interest, we shall simply list some of the more important events.

In 499 B.C. Greek cities in Ionia revolted, and in the following year, with aid from Athens and Eritria, they attacked and burned Sardis.[13]

The rebellions were presently put down. In 490 B.C., an expedition of perhaps twenty thousand men was sent under Datis and Artaphernes to punish Eritria and Athens. Eritria fell after a siege of six days. In Attica, they disembarked at Marathon to await word about a revolt in Athens they had hoped to foment. They presently embarked their cavalry, preparing to set sail against Athens. Miltiades, the Greek general,

116

seized this chance to attack. Though outnumbered, the Greeks were victorious. They promptly marched to Athens. They reached there ahead of the Persians, who abandoned the expedition.[14]

In 481 B.C., Xerxes I led an expedition against Greece. He had an army estimated at 150,000 men and a navy of perhaps 660 mercenary triremes. The army, because of its size, had to go by land but stay near the coast so that it could be provisioned by sea. Between Thessaly and Locris, there was a narrow pass it had to go through at Thermopylae. This was guarded by Spartan "Equals." It took the Persians two days and cost them many men to force their way through this pass; they killed all the "Equals."[15]

The Persians easily overran Attica. The Athenian army moved south, most of them to the island of Salamis. Some Greek generals thought the Greeks should fall back to the Isthmus of Corinth to make a stand; Themistocles, who was in command of the Athenian forces, thought there should be a naval battle. The Persians now had about 340 triremes; the Greeks about 300. Somehow the Persian fleet was led to attack the Greeks in the Strait of Salamis. The Greeks drew them into the narrower part of the strait; hand-to-hand conflict followed. The Athenians had hoplites aboard; the Persians were routed, 480 B.C.[16]

Most of the Persians went home; a substantial force wintered in Greece. In the spring these Persians were ravaging Attica. When they heard a Greek army was after them, they withdrew to Boeotia. In the battle of Plataea, 479 B.C., the Greeks were victorious. At about this time, too, a Greek force captured a Persian camp at Mycale on the eastern coast of the Aegean Sea, ending Persian naval power in the area.[17]

Under Athenian leadership, an organization called the Delian League was formed, c. 478 B.C. Most of the member states were islands in the Aegean. It shortly became the Athenian naval empire. From its inception to c. 449 B.C., it was engaged in wars with Persia. In 449 B.C., an agreement between King Artaxerxes I and the Delian League ended the

Graeco-Persian war.[18]
Despite the fact that the Persians never succeeded in conquering Greece, they continued to have a great Empire.

Notes

Section VI.

1. Georges Roux, *Ancient Iraq* (Harmondsworth, Middlesex, England: Penguin Books 1966, first published by George Allen & Unwin, 1964), p. 313; Chester G. Starr, *A History of the Ancient World* (New York: Oxford University Press, 1965), p. 138.

2. Roux, *Ancient Iraq,* pp. 340–42; Starr, *Ancient World,* p. 138; Cyrus H. Gordon, *The Ancient Near East,* rev. ed.(New York: W. W. Norton & Co., 1965; originally published as *The World of the Old Testament,* Ventnor Publishers, 1953), pp. 254–55; *Encyclopaedia Britannica,* 1929, vol. 2, p. 857; vol. 15, p. 172; vol. 17, p. 567.

3. Roux, *Ancient Iraq,* p. 343; Starr, *Ancient World,* p. 139; Gordon, *The Ancient Near East* p. 255.

4. Roux, *Ancient Iraq,* pp. 343–45; Starr, *Ancient World,* p. 151; Gordon, *The Ancient Near East,* pp. 259–60, 262–63; *Encyclopedia Britannica,* 1968, vol. 2, p. 967.

5. Roux, *Ancient Iraq,* pp. 338, 355–60; Gordon, *The Ancient Near East,* pp. 259–60; *Encyclopaedia Britannica,* 1929, vol. 2, pp. 851–52; vol. 22, p. 885; vol. 23, p. 525; *Encyclopaedia Britannica,* 1968, vol. 2, p. 967; vol. 18, p. 454; vol. 22, p. 775.

6. Neugebauer,"Ancient Mathematics and Astronomy," in *A History of Technology,* eds. Charles Singer, E. J. Holmyard, and A. R. Hall (Oxford: Oxford University Press, 1954), vol. 1, pp. 793ff.; Roux, *Ancient Iraq,* pp. 331–33, 338, 354, 375; J. A. de Gobineau, *The World of the Persians* (Geneva: Editions Minerva, 1971), p. 43; Pierre Grimal, *Hellenism and the Rise of Rome* (New York: Delacorte Press, 1965), pp. 3, 285–87.

7. Roux, *Ancient Iraq,* pp. 348–53, 366, 373; Starr, *Ancient World,* p. 140; Gordon, *The Ancient Near East,* pp. 26, 265, 269, 299; de Gobineau, *Persians,* pp. 33, 50–51; *Encyclopaedia Britannica,* 1929, vol. 4, p. 655; vol. 17, p. 567; *Encyclopaedia Britannica,* 1968, vol. 2, p. 659; vol. 17, p. 656.

8. Roux, *Ancient Iraq,* pp. 370–71; Gordon, *The Ancient Near East,* pp. 272–73; deGobineau, *Persians,* p. 50; *Encyclopaedia Britannica,* 1929, vol. 4, p. 655; vol. 8, p. 76; Herodotus, *The History,* trans. George Rawlinson (London: J. M. Dent and Sons, Ltd.; New York: E. P. Dutton & Co., 1910), book III, chaps. 11–13, 64, 66.

9. Gordon, *The Ancient Near East,* p. 283; J. F. C. Fuller, *The Generalship of Alexander the Great* (New York: Funk & Wagnalls, 1968 paperback; published by arrangement with Rutgers University Press), pp. 77–78; de Gobineau, *Persians,* pp. 76, 81; S. M. Cole, "Roads," in *A History of Technology,* eds. Charles Singer, E. J. Holmyard, and A. R. Hall (New York: Oxford University

118

Press, 1954), vol. 1, p. 713; Xenophon, *Anabasis*, rev. ed., edited and with an introduction by William W. Goodwin and John Williams White; Greek-English dictionary by John Williams White and Morris H. Morgan (Boston: Ginn & Co., 1894), p. xiv; Herodotus, *The History*, book V, chaps. 52, 53.

10. deGobineau, *Persians*, p. 43; *Encyclopaedia Britannica*, 1968, vol. 21, p. 604.

11. Fuller, *Alexander the Great*, pp. 164, 166–167; Starr, *Ancient World*, p. 399; Xenophon, *Anabasis*, dictionary, p. 60.

12. Thucidides, *The History of the Peloponnesian War*, trans. Richard Crawley (London: J. M. Dent and Sons, Ltd., 1910), pp. 310–11.

13. Starr, *Ancient World*, p. 282; *Encyclopaedia Britannica*, 1929, vol. 10, pp. 591, 769; Catherine B. Avery, ed., *The New Century Classical Handbook* (New York: Appleton-Century-Crofts, 1962), pp. 155, 857–58; Herodotus, *The History*, book V, chaps. 97–101.

14. Starr, *Ancient World*, pp. 283–85; Avery, *Classical Handbook*, pp. 673, 715, 858; *Encyclopaedia Britannica*, 1929, vol. 10, pp. 592–93; Herodotus, *The History*, book V, chap. 124; book VI, especially chaps. 18, 94, 101, 110, 112–116.

15. Starr, *Ancient World*, pp. 288–89; Avery, *Classical Handbook*, pp. 859, 1080; *Encyclopaedia Britannica*, 1929, vol. 10, p. 549; Herodotus, *The History*, book VII, chaps. 222–226.

16. Starr, *Ancient World*, pp. 389–90; Avery, *Classical Handbook*, pp. 859, 974–75; *Encyclopaedia Britannica*, 1929, vol. 10, pp. 593–95; Herodotus, *The History*, book VIII, especially chaps. 40, 42, 51, 74–76, 82–86, 115.

17. Starr, *Ancient World*, pp. 291–92; Avery, *Classical Handbook*, pp. 729, 859, 899; *Encyclopaedia Britannica*, 1929, vol. 10, pp. 595–96; vol. 21, p. 171; Herodotus, *The History*, book VIII, chaps. 131, 143; book IX, especially chaps. 11–15, 23, 57–65, 100–103.

18. Starr, *Ancient World*, pp. 292–94; Avery, *Classical Handbook*, pp. 371, 859; *Encyclopaedia Britannica*, 1929, vol. 7, pp. 164–66; vol. 10, p. 596.

Section VII. Alexander and His Empire

In spite of the Greek civil war, 431–404 B.C., and the fact that long after it was over there was still no unity among Greek city-states, during the fourth century B.C., Greeks were becoming increasingly influential in Persian affairs. In 380 B.C., the Athenian orator, Isocrates, in his oration Panegyricus, argued for a Kulturkrieg against the Empire, and there was some sympathy for this proposal. In 337 B.C., King Philip II of Macedonia had achieved a dominant position in the Greek world; he had organized it into a league against Persia, the league of Corinth. This included all the mainland city-states except Sparta and a number of the Aegean islands. A year later he was in process of starting an expedition against Persia when he was assassinated. His son, Alexander III, Alexander the Great, ascended the throne at the age of twenty. He held views similar to those of his father.[1]

Alexander had first to establish himself as hegemon (generalissimo) of the League. This meant an expedition south through Thessaly and Boeotia as far as Thebes, though it involved no fighting. He had next, in 335 B.C., to conduct a difficult campaign in Thrace and Illyria. Then he had to put down the revolt of a member of the League, Thebes. Thebes was ruthlessly destroyed. When Alexander set forth on his expedition into Asia, he left a trusted general, Antipater, as deputy generalissimo of the League to look after things while he was away.[2]

It seems clear that the League of Corinth was organized to join together the city-states of Greece and the kingdom of Macedonia in an alliance that was to conduct a war against Persia. Philip had advertised it as a war to avenge the desecration by Xerxes of Greek temples and sanctuaries in 481 B.C., but this was probably not all that he had had in mind. When Alexander, in 334 B.C., set out on his expedition into Asia allegedly to avenge the wrongs committed by Xerxes, he probably had no idea how far this expedition might take him. But the noncombat personnel he took with him included a number of professional people, physicians, surveyors, a geographer, an historian, and an architect. There was also a secretarial staff that wrote the Journal, the daily official record of the expedition. And Alexander took with him a great deal of learning. He had been tutored for three years by Aristotle. He must have been well informed about the civilizations of western Asia and Egypt, and about the current status of the physical and biological sciences, also about recent developments in military technology.[3]

The army of invasion with which Alexander started out included thirty thousand infantry, five thousand cavalry, and perhaps five thousand auxiliaries, principally engineers and his quartermaster service. The size of his army was probably limited by financial and political considerations; he was not in a position to afford additional mercenaries, and he did not think it would be wise to have too large a Greek contingent. Macedonians probably made up something like half his total fighting force.[4]

Shortly after Alexander entered Anatolia, he met a Persian army in the battle of the Granicus. He had a narrow escape, but he won a signal victory. The Persian losses included a son-in-law of Darius, three satraps, and several important army officers.

As Alexander's expedition moved forward on the path he had chosen for it for reasons perhaps mainly of military strategy, he was taking over one piece of territory after another. He must quite soon have recognized two problems that he had to deal with, a personnel problem and a political problem. The former was whom to appoint to govern the territories he was taking over. The latter was how to enlist sufficient support for the governments he was establishing by making these appointments.

At first the political problem was easy to solve. In Ionia, he could afford to leave the Greek city-states to govern themselves; he had liberated them. The Phoenician city-states, except for Tyre, he left also to govern themselves, though in this case he appointed a Macedonian to collect tribute. For Egypt and Babylonia, the problem was more complicated, but in both cases one thing he did was to take a cue from Cyrus. In Egypt he offered sacrifice to Apis and other Egyptian gods, he became a pharaoh (this meant he was deified), and he visited the oracle of Ammon at Siwah. In Babylon he worshipped Marduk, and he directed the restoration of Marduk's temple. In both places his takeover was welcomed. To deal with the political problem in Persia, Alexander treated various high Persian officials as friends and allies, demanded that they pay him the same homage they had paid Darius—perform the ceremony of prostration—and began wearing Persian apparel. A number of high-ranking Macedonian officers resented these moves. One result of this resentment was that situations developed in which Alexander committed what have been called his personal misdeeds—the murder of Cleitus, the execution of Callisthenes, and the assassination at his order of Pharmenio. Another was a mutiny at Opis in 323 B.C. that Alexander succeeded in converting presently into a feast at which he offered prayer for peace and for partnership between Macedonians and Persians.[5]

Another way Alexander dealt with his political problem was through marriage. In 328 B.C., he married Roxane, the daughter of Oxyartes, a Sogdian baron whose stronghold in Turkestan he was trying to take. Alexander and Oxyartes became allies. In 324 B.C., he arranged a mass marriage ceremony in which many of his Macedonian generals and soldiers married Persian and Median wives. He himself married Barsine, a daughter of Darius.[6]

The personnel problem was partly one of the number of Macedonians he could afford to leave behind him as he advanced eastward. It is true that at Susa he received a reinforcement of several thousand fresh Macedonian troops. But he had had battle and other losses, and he could expect to have more. Moreover, despite the fact that with the gold and silver he had captured at Persepolis and Susa he was no longer limited by a shortage of funds in the number of mercenaries he could hire, he nonetheless needed to keep his Macedonia force largely intact.[7]

The other side of the personnel problem was whom, other

than Macedonians, he could trust. He decided in Persia to trust a number of Persians. His first major Persian appointment was Mazaeus, the general who had proved to be his principal opponent in the battle of Arbela. He made Mazaeus satrap of Babylonia. After that, quite a number of other Persians were appointed to rule other Persian satrapies. Of course, his policy of treating Persians as friends and allies was aimed at making these satraps his loyal subjects. How he handled the situation in Sogdiana has already been indicated. In India, he left each of two rival rajahs, Taxiles and Porus, to rule a substantial area. Even if some of his non-Madedonian appointees—and, likewise, some Macedonians—abused their trusts, this was perhaps on the whole the wisest way of dealing with the personnel problem that was open to him. But it should be pointed out that, wherever feasible, he divided the functions of government and retained strategic functions in Macedonian hands. Thus, in Babylonia, he put a Macedonian general in charge of the Babylonian military force and appointed another Macedonian to collect the taxes.[8]

In 330 and early 329 B.C., Alexander went to Susa and Persepolis, the two great Persian capitals, then to nearby Pasargadae, and then to Ecbatana. Before he left Ecbatana the nature of his expedition had undergone a major change. At Persepolis, he burned the palace of Xerxes; thereafter, the expedition no longer had any claim to a revenge objective. During the winter at Persepolis he heard that Antipater had defeated the Spartans in a hard-fought battle and that Sparta had joined the League of Corinth. But the League had ceased to be important to Alexander. At Ecbatana he paid off the Greeks and the Thessalians and sent them home with a bonus of two thousand talents. At Susa, Persepolis, and Pasargadae, all told he had captured a vast amount of hoarded silver and gold. At Susa, according to the 1968 edition of *Encyclopaedia Brittannica,* he had captured some fifty thousand talents of gold. What he captured at Persepolis is thought to have been a larger hoard. If we take one talent to be equal to 57.75 pounds avoirdupois, the Susa hoard of gold presumably weighed about 46 million ounces.[9]

One consequence of capturing all this gold and silver was that from Ecbatana onward Alexander made increasing use of mercenaries.

It is difficult to characterize what Alexander did that improved military technology and the methods of warfare, largely because his successes resulted to an important extent from his personal traits. He was a daring, even foolhardy, soldier who had several narrow personal escapes. On more than one occasion, he drove himself and his men almost to the point of exhaustion in order to move with sufficient speed to take his enemy by surprise. And when he was told that something was impossible, he proceeded to find a way to do it. Moreover, he had an astounding ability to vary his tactics to make them appropriate to cope in turn with each of the various types of enemy he encountered.[10]

Another factor to which a number of his successes were largely due that complicates an attempt to appraise his contributions to military technology and methods of warfare is the excellence of the noncombat units of his army, his engineer corps, and his quartermaster service. Perhaps it will be best to give some illustrations.

1. The catapult had long been used as a siege engine. Alexander seems to have been the first to use it as a field artillery piece.[11]

2. In the siege of Tyre and, also, that of Massaga in India, Alexander had a bridge or corvus equipped mechanically so that it could be lowered onto an enemy's breached city wall to permit his storming troops to rush over it.[12]

3. In the siege of Tyre, Alexander undertook to build a causeway out to the island city over which he could move his siege towers. The causeway had to be about half a mile long. At places, it was two hundred feet wide. Although it was apparently not quite completed when the city capitulated, the size of the undertaking and the speed with which it was pushed make it a very impressive engineering feat. Not long after Alexander took Tyre, he laid siege to Gaza. This fortress was

built on a hill. To make it possible to attack the wall with battering-rams, he had to build up a level approach. General J. F. C. Fuller thought this construction job may have been more difficult than building the causeway at Tyre, but it must have been completed very quickly. This siege lasted only about two months.[13]

4. The siege towers Alexander had at Tyre were said to be 150 feet high. There were two of them. They had to be manipulated out over the causeway. Also, since the Tyrians succeeded in burning them, they had to be replaced. This construction and manipulation was another impressive engineering feat.[14]

5. The Tyrian city wall at the point approached by the causeway was so strong and so strongly defended that Alexander decided to try attacking it at other points. This meant mounting a ram on a boat, or perhaps on two or more boats lashed together, or else on a long scow constructed for the purpose or on a platform supported on pontoons. No one else seems ever to have used a battering-ram on any kind of float. Whatever the nature of Alexander's float, it had to be placed against the city wall and firmly anchored there. Presumably, it had a testudo roof. Alexander succeeded in finding a place in the Tyrian wall that he could breach with his ram mounted on the float his engineers had devised to support it. The combination of this breach and his fleet—he had over three hundred ships—made it possible for him to take Tyre. Tyre collapsed after a siege of seven months.[15]

6. Aornus was a mountain fortress west of the upper Indus River that Alexander besieged in 326 B.C. The top of the mountain was an arable plateau. Its elevation was some 7,100 feet. The only feasible approach to Aornus was across a ravine. Alexander was able to camp on the other side of this ravine at a place the elevation of which was about 6,750 feet. Across the ravine from his camp was a shoulder of Aornus of about the same elevation. The distance from his camp to this shoulder was roughly five hundred yards; the shoulder was out of the range of his catapults and bowmen. The bottom of the ravine

was some 450 feet below his camp. There was plenty of timber, and Alexander ordered the construction of what seems to have been a trestle. The trestle was apparently sufficiently completed in five days to permit a storming party to cross over to Aornus on it and capture the fortress.[16]

7. Before the battle of the Hydaspes, Porus was encamped on the southeast side of the river, Alexander on the northwest side, at a place some 130 miles southeast of Peshawar. The river was perhaps a mile wide. Alexander wanted to cross the river at night and take Porus by surprise. But for a considerable distance along the river, Porus had pickets posted at each possible ford; and with the pickets were elephants that would make taking cavalry across very difficult. Alexander feinted crossing attempts for a number of nights until he thought Porus was off his guard. During this period Alexander assembled his fleet of ships and rafts. He seems to have had a number of ships taken apart at a point on the Indus River, transported a distance of more than a hundred miles, and then put back together again. He also had a large number of smaller boats and probably several hundred rafts made by stuffing skins with hay. His fleet was apparently hidden at a point some eighteen miles upstream from the place where the battle was fought. On the chosen night, he loaded five thousand horses and fifteen thousand men onto the boats and rafts, and took them several miles downstream to what he thought was a suitable landing place on the southeastern shore. It proved to be an island so his horses and men had to wade ashore through water perhaps more than four feet deep and then to overcome the Indian picket force that was on guard at that point. The crossing was successful, although Porus learned about it while it was in process. Apparently, if he had promptly attacked with his main army, the result might have been less favorable for Alexander. As it was, Alexander won the battle. General J. F. C. Fuller says of the crossing that "the staff work of the Macedonian army must have been superb."[17]

Alexander had apparently wanted to take all of India, which he had thought did not extend eastward very far beyond the battlefield on the Hydaspes. He pushed eastward perhaps another 180 miles to a point on the Beas River. Here, in 326 B.C., during the heat of the summer and the wet of the monsoon his army mutinied. Probably by this time, contacts with Indians had somewhat corrected his geographical misconceptions. Moreover, his communication line had become very long, and he must have realized that there was an increasing number of problems about the loyalty of men to whom he had delegated the control of various parts of his empire. At all events, he yielded to his men and agreed to give up the idea of pushing farther east.[18]

Some of the things Alexander did that have no close connection with military technology or improvements in government organization should probably be noted in concluding these comments on him. He was a great founder of cities and trading posts. He founded at least seventeen Alexandrias. The most famous one was in Egypt; all the others save one were east of the Tigris River. He ordered the improvement of the harbors of Patala and Babylon to provide better communication between India and Persia. He had the gold and silver captured at Persepolis and elsewhere coined. And he found various ways to get the coins into circulation. He gave gifts to his generals and soldiers and gave generous dowries to the brides who were married at the mass-marriage ceremony at Susa. It is reasonable to suppose that putting something like 250,000 talents worth of new money into circulation promoted the spread of money transactions and stimulated trade and productive activity.[19]

Early in June 323 B.C., at Babylon, Alexander contracted a fever, perhaps malaria; on the thirteenth he died.[20]

Notes

Section VII.

1. Chester G. Starr, *A History of the Ancient World* (New York: Oxford University Press, 1965), pp. 371, 375; Major General J.F.C. Fuller, *The Generalship of Alexander the Great* (New York: Funk & Wagnalls, 1968 paperback;

published by arrangement with Rutgers University Press), pp. 31–32, 36–38, 46, 89–90; *Encyclopaedia Britannica,* 1929, vol. 1, p. 567; vol. 12, pp. 18–19; vol. 17, pp. 57–73; *Encyclopaedia Britannica,* 1968, vol. 1, pp. 571–72.

2. Fuller, *Alexander the Great,* pp. 82–88; *Encyclopaedia Britannica,* 1929, vol. 1, p. 567; *Encyclopaedia Britannica,* 1968, vol. 1, p. 572; vol. 2, p. 79; Catherine B. Avery, ed., *The New Century Classical Handbook* (New York: Appleton-Century-Crofts, Inc., 1962), p. 74.

3. Starr, *Ancient World,* p. 382; Fuller, *Alexander the Great,* pp. 52, 56–57; *Encyclopaedia Britannica,* 1929, vol. 1, p. 567; *Encyclopaedia Britannica,* 1968, vol. 1, p. 571; vol. 2, p. 391.

4. Starr, *Ancient World,* p. 397; Fuller, *Alexander the Great,* pp. 49–53; *Encyclopaedia Britannica,* 1929, vol. 1, p. 567; *Encyclopaedia Britannica,* 1968, vol. 2, p. 445; Avery, *Classicial Handbook,* p. 75.

5. Fuller, *Alexander the Great,* pp. 64–68, 105, 107–8, 114, 272; Victor Tcherikover, *Hellenistic Civilization and the Jews* (New York: Atheneum, 1959), p. 45; Starr, *Ancient World,* pp. 398, 401–2; *Encyclopaedia Britannica,* 1968, vol. 1, pp. 573–75.

6. Fuller, *Alexander the Great,* pp. 122, 137, 244, 271, 274; Starr, *Ancient World,* p. 403; *Encyclopaedia Britannica,* 1929, vol. 1, p. 570; *Encyclopaedia Britannica,* 1968, vol. 1, pp. 574, 575; vol. 8, p. 56.

7. Fuller, *Alexander the Great,* pp. 269, 271.

8. Fuller, *Alexander the Great,* pp. 59, 109, 124–26, 128–29, 267, 270–71; *Encyclopaedia Britannica,* 1929, vol. 1, p. 570; *Encyclopaedia Britannica,* 1968, vol. 1, pp. 572, 575.

9. Fuller, *Alexander the Great,* pp. 112, 273–74; *Encyclopaedia Britannica,* 1929, vol. 1, p. 568; vol. 17, p. 611; *Encyclopaedia Britannica,* 1968, vol. 1, p. 573.

10. Fuller, *Alexander the Great,* pp. 97, 132–33, 153, 156, 238–39, 261–63; *Encyclopaedia Britannica,* 1968, vol. 1, pp. 575–76. The battle formation Alexander devised to deal with the Scythians is of particular interest. They were a nomadic people, skilled horsemen, who fought more or less as individuals, avoiding any concentration of their forces that could be overcome in a mass operation. Alexander enticed them into a concentration.

11. Fuller, *Alexander the Great,* p. 296; *Encyclopaedia Britannica,* 1968, vol. 1, p. 574.

12. Fuller, *Alexander the Great,* pp. 215, 246.

13. Starr, *Ancient World,* p. 398; Fuller, *Alexander the Great,* pp. 104, 208–9, 217–18; Tcherikover, *Hellenistic Civilization,* pp. 41, 50; *Encyclopaedia Britannica,* 1929, vol. 17, p. 768; vol. 22, p. 563; *Encyclopaedia Britannica,* 1968, vol. 1, p. 573; vol. 22, p. 452.

14. Fuller, *Alexander the Great,* pp. 210–11; *Encyclopaedia Britannica,* 1929, vol. 22, p. 563.

15. Fuller, *Alexander the Great,* pp. 212, 214–16; *Encyclopaedia Britannica,* 1929, vol. 17, p. 768; vol. 22, p. 563; *Encyclopedia Brittanica,* 1968, vol. 1, p. 573, vol. 22, p. 452.

16. Fuller, *Alexander the Great,* p. 127; *Encyclopaedia Britannica,* 1929, vol. 2, p. 90.

17. Fuller, *Alexander the Great,* pp. 128, 183–99; *Encyclopaedia Britannica,* 1968, vol. 11, p. 922.

18. Starr, *Ancient World*, p. 401; Fuller, *Alexander the Great*, pp. 129–31; *Encyclopaedia Britannica*, 1968, vol. 1, p. 574.

19. Fuller, *Alexander the Great*, pp. 105, 133, 273–74, 291; Starr, *Ancient World*, 402, 403, 408; *Encyclopaedia Britannica*, 1968, vol. 8, p. 82.

20. Fuller, *Alexander the Great*, p. 143; *Encyclopaedia Brittanica*, 1929, vol. 1, p. 570; *Encyclopaedia Britannica*, 1968, vol. 1, p. 575.

Chapter V

Foreign Exchange in
the Eastern Mediterranean
in the Fourth Century B.C.

Probably all through the fourth century B.C. there was extensive intercommunity trade in the eastern Mediterranean Sea.[1]

The local sources of gold, silver, and copper in this area were beginning to be somewhat worked out. However, in Macedonia, Philip II had "major gold mines at Mt. Pangaeus," there were apparently still some rich silver-lead ore veins in Laurium, and copper was still an important export for Cyprus. But Spain had become a leading source for all three of these metals.[2] Tin came from Cornwall and Brittany via Gadir (Cadiz) and Carthage.[3] There were iron mines in various places; the Chaldi, or Chalybes, a people of the Pontus, were famous ironsmiths, noted for the near steel that they produced.[4]

The grain raised in Egypt and Cyrenaica and in the Crimea and in Sicily was a major food-source for Athens, Corinth and Delos, and for several Ionian cities.[5] Laodicea and various Greek cities on the eastern Mediterranean were famous for the wines that they produced.[6] There was also substantial intercommunity trading in olive oil, dried figs, dates, and other foodstuffs.[7]

Miletus was a major manufacturing center. It was the most important exporter of woolen goods. Linen came principally

130

from Egypt. Cos was famous not only as the birthplace of Hippocrates and for its medical school but also for its silks and the diaphanous feminine garments made from them.[8]

Practically all papyrus came from Egypt. Several areas exported pitch and bitumen, among them Macedonia, the Troad, and Babylonia.[9] The most famous marbles came from Mt. Pentelicus in Attica and the island of Paros.[10] Lumber was exported from various places, cedar from Lebanon, pine from Cyprus and Macedonia, oak from Bashan, and so on.[11] Tyre was the leading trading center of Phoenicia. It was famous for the purple dye and dyed goods it produced.[12] Arabian exports included frankincense, myrrh, and precious stones.[13] This listing of commodities traded in does not pretend to be at all complete, and, of course, the listing of importers and exporters is very sketchy. One other commodity should certainly be mentioned, slaves. Little is known about how large the volume of the slave trade was in the fourth century, but some slave trade there certainly was. Three men that are mentioned below, Hermias, Pasio, and Phormio, each spent the early years of his life as a slave.

For one city-state, Athens, we can say something about the volume of its foreign trade and about its balance of international payments. We know that Attica was heavily dependent on imports for its food, although farming was still a major industry. George M. Calhoun estimates that "the annual importation of grain probably averaged well over a million bushels."[14] Athens also imported a large quantity of another agricultural product, olives. These came from the great groves in the valley below Delphi. For the most part, they were made into olive oil, and most of the oil was exported.[15] Another important export was pottery, although Athens no longer dominated the pottery-manufacturing industry, as it had in the late sixth and in the fifth centuries. Athens also exported honey, figs, and some metal and textile products. Piraeus had a fortified harbor, and merchants from Asia Minor and Syria found it a safe and convenient place to stop off and break a voyage.[16]

Athens levied a tax of 2% on its imports and exports,

and the yield of this tax gives us important information about the volume of Athenian external trade. In 401 B.C. the yield was some 200,000 drachmas or 33⅓ talents.[17] This, on the basis of the weight of an Athenian drachma, is equivalent to about 30,000 ounces of silver, but the current value of this much silver does not provide a very helpful comparison. E. Victor Morgan suggests a more meaningful one. The daily wage of a skilled craftsman in the middle of the fourth century was about one drachma, and his annual income was perhaps 300 to 325 drachmas.[18] Things were probably not very different in 401 B.C. This would make the yield of the 2% tax in that year the equivalent of the annual earnings of five or six hundred craftsmen.

There are doubtless various other items in the Athenian balance of international payments beside the imports and exports noted above, items about which information is for the most part lacking. We assume that in any year in which there was a more than negligible deficit, Athens made it up by a payment in silver; and that in any year in which there was a surplus of consequence, Athens received from the rest of the commercial world a payment in silver of the amount of the surplus.

Quite possibly, there were transactions other than balance-settling transactions involving exports of silver. The mines of Laurium that had produced so much silver in the early years of the fifth century had become less productive, and during the latter part of the Peloponnesian War, mining operations had become negligible. After the war recovery was not very prompt. During the latter half of the fourth century, however, silver production increased. At least during this period Athens may have exported silver manufactures.[19]

By 400 B.C., "there was a very large number of cities and states each with their own coinage."[20] We assume that for each of these polities there was a separate balance of its international payments, and that a business transaction between any two of them required a foreign exchange conversion from the currency circulating in one to the currency circulating in the other. Most such transactions arose out of foreign trade, one polity importing merchandise from another. But there were also nonmerchandise transactions. One of these after Plato's death (348 or 347 B.C.) is of some interest.[21] Aristotle, since he was not an Athenian citizen, could not hold title to the Academy grounds.[22] He had no strong reason for staying in Athens. He was invited by his friend and former pupil, Hermias, who was then the ruler of Assus and Atarneus, to come to Assus as his guest. So Aristotle moved there. Presumably he converted the Athenian owls that he held into the currency of Assus.[23]

We have been making implicitly an assumption that at this point it would be best to make explicit. A great volume of international settlements was made each year, probably amounting to ten million drachmas or more annually in the case of Athens. For the most part these settlements were made without shipments of specie. As Morgan points out, "The cost of transporting the precious metals and the risk of robbery gave a strong incentive to find other means of making international payments."[24] A major factor because of which it was advisable to avoid specie shipments whenever possible was piracy. During a part of the fifth century, the dominance of the Athenian navy in the Eastern Mediterranean did a good deal to keep piracy in check, and during much of the third, the Rhodesian navy performed a similar service. But in the fourth century, in spite of the fact that Sidon, and Tyre until 332, had strong navies, piracy seems to have been for the most part unrestrained.[25]

Largely avoiding specie shipments was clearly advisable. It was clearly advisable, also, when men travelled, that they should avoid carrying much money on their persons. The case of a man called Protus, whose trip from Athens to Syracuse is reported in one of the quotations from orations written by Demosthenes given in Exhibit B, is of interest in this connection. Protus borrowed money in Athens which he used in Syracuse to purchase a quantity of grain. The captain of the ship on which he travelled, Hegestratus, and a fellow passenger, Zenothemis, planned an elaborate swindle, about which more will be said shortly. For the moment, it will suffice to note that, if Protus had carried on his person in the form of specie the money that he spent in Syracuse, Hegestratus would simply have robbed him.[26]

What has been said above about foreign exhange implies that converting the kind of money circulating in Polity A into the kind circulating in Polity B did not usually involve a physical money-changer operation. It seems to be agreed that by 400 B.C. the business of exchanging coins issued by Polity A for coins issued by Polity B had evolved into the banking business. There was still a need for money changing in the sense of coin exchanging. As Morgan says, it was one of the "functions of bankers in the Greek city states." And he goes on to say that "the name for them (trapezetai) is derived from the tables . . . used for exchanging coins."[27] But we incline to think that by the fourth century coin exchanging had become a minor function of a Greek bank.

By that time, accepting deposits, lending money at interest, and making payments on behalf of the bank's clients had become major banking functions, also acting as surety for a client and serving as a custodian of wills, contracts, and other documents.[28] Two further functions that were performed by at least one Athenian bank should be mentioned, acting as a pawnbroker and providing a safety-deposit service. [29] We contend that there was still another function of Greek banks, a very important one in the fourth century, that of providing foreign exchange in a way that largely avoided specie shipments. We propose the hypothesis that they did this through a type of credit instrument developed for the purpose, a kind of sight draft drawn by a banker in one polity on a banker in another.

In support of this hypothesis, we cite the various instances in which a man borrowed money in one place, apparently took some evidence of this with him on a journey to another place (but did not carry the money on his person), and had the money to spend in that other place on his arrival there.[30] The instances we cite make it seem likely that the type of transaction involved was an extremely common one. Indeed, what Calhoun has to say about the Athenian grain trade makes it appear that almost every bushel of grain imported into Athens in the fourth century was imported under a contract like that between Protus and Demo, who lent him the money for his expedition, what is called a respondentia contract. Calhoun says that the lender in one of these contracts was usually a resident of Athens (i.e., the loan was made in Athens), and the borrower was obligated to use the money at a specified export port to buy a specified quantity of wheat or other grain and to have the grain transported from this port to Athens and marketed there.[31]

The swindle planned by Hegestratus and Zenothemis should now be explained. Both were citizens of Massalia (Marseilles). When the grain that Protus had bought on his arrival at Syracuse had been loaded on the ship, they claimed that Zenothemis owned it, and at Syracuse they borrowed money on it as security and immediately sent this money to Massalia. The Greek word translated as "sent" here is the aorist of ἀποστέλλω, a word that was used in connection with the sending of a message or the dispatching of a messenger. It certainly does not suggest a shipment of specie. It seems reasonable to suppose that the money was sent for deposit in a bank in Massalia.[32]

But a fuller statement of the hypothesis we propose is called for. We assume that any banker who did a foreign exchange business entered into correspondent relationships with bankers in other places. We further assume that a banker in Polity A would have a deposit in the bank of his correspondent in Polity B, or else the correspondent would have a deposit balance in the bank in Polity A. Thus, when a client of a banker in Polity A wanted to convert some of his Polity A currency into Polity B currency, he would pay the banker in Polity A for a sight draft on the banker in Polity B. The draft would result in a debit to the balance of the Polity A banker in the Polity B bank, or alternatively in a credit to the balance of the Polity B banker in the Polity A bank. One further feature of the hypothesis we propose should be noted: we assume that in any currency conversion of the sort we have been considering each of the two bankers made a charge for his service. The charge probably ordinarily amounted to no more than a small fraction of one percent of the money converted.

We believe a passage in one of the orations written by Demosthenes cited in Exhibit B gives support to the assumption of such a charge, Apollodorus v. Polycles.[33] Appolodorus had continued acting as a tierarch beyond his appointed time because Polycles, appointed as his successor, had not taken over. In this suit, Apollodorus was seeking reimbursement for various expenses his overtime service had involved. Concerning these expenses, he said that he "had written down not only the disbursements themselves but also the objects for which the money had been spent . . . in the coinage of what country the payment had been made, and what the loss in exchange was." The last six words are a translation of these Greek words: ὁπόσυ ἡ καταλλογὴ ἦ τῶ ἀργυρίῳ. We think that a better translation would be "the cost of the foreign exchange" and that these six Greek words provide support for including a foreign exchange in our hypothesis.

The hypothesis here proposed explains what seems to have been a very frequent three-step sequence of events in the fourth century and probably before that, also. It explains how a man could (1) have in one place money of the kind circulating there, (2) travel a good many miles to another place, and (3) have this money converted into the currency circulating in that other place and be able to spend it there. This was a sequence of events in which the money may be said to have been transported from the place where the traveller had it to begin with to the place where he spent it by a method of transportation that did not involve the movement of this money in the form of specie from one place to the other. We assume that the traveller carried, not specie on his person, but a negotiable instrument, a sight draft drawn by his banker, and that this draft was drawn on a correspondent banker in the place where the traveller had the money to spend. Our hypothesis explains the frequent three-step sequence of events. No satisfactory alternative explanation seems to have been proposed.

Exhibit A

Note on Athenian Currency*

1 talent = 60 minas
1 mina = 100 drachmas
1 drachma = 6 obols

4.37 grams of silver, or .154 of an ounce, had the value of one drachma.

The four-drachma coin had a picture of an owl stamped on one face. Hence the tetradrachm coins came to be referred to as owls.

Exhibit B

Selected Private Orations Written by Demosthenes†

Quote I. Apollodorus vs Phormio, Vol. VI No. XXXVI. A Friend Speaking for Phormio.
Pasio had been a slave; he had won his freedom. The same was true of Phormio. [48]

*From *Webster's New International Dictionary of the English Language,* 2nd ed., unabridged (Springfield, Mass.: G. and G. Merriam Company, 1947), pp. 1562, 1680, 1745, 2898.
†Direct and indirect quotations from Demosthenes, *Private Orations,* trans. A. T. Murray (Cambridge: Harvard University Press, vol. 4, 1936, vol. 5 and 6, 1939).

"The real property of Pasio was about 20 talents, but in addition to this he had more than 50 talents in money of his own lent out at interest. Among these were 11 talents of the bank's deposits, profitably invested." Phormio "leased the business of the bank and took over the deposits, realizing that, if he had not yet obtained the right of citizenship . . . . he would not be able to recover the moneys that Pasio had lent on the security of land and lodging houses, he chose to have Pasio himself as the debtor for these sums, rather than the others to whom he had lent them. It was for this reason that Pasio was set down as owing 11 talents." [5, 6]

Phormio had operated the bank and the shield factory left by Pasio for 8 years under a lease. The bank was leased for 10 years to Xeno, Euphraeus, Euphro, and Callistratus. [37, 38]

The suit with which this oration is concerned was instituted 18 or 20 years after Pasio's death. [Introduction]

After these leases Apollodorus and his brother, Pasicles, divided the estate they had inherited from their father, Pasio. Apollodorus took the shield factory, Pasicles the bank. The factory yielded an income of one talent, the bank an income of one talent 40 minas. The factory was thought to involve less risk. [11]

Apollodorus had received a lodging house under his father's will, because he was the elder son. [34]

During the 8 years of Phormio's operation of the bank and the factory Apollodorus had received one talent 20 minas per year, one half the total rent. [37, 51]

"Pasio is set down in the lease as debtor to the bank, not as having given capital to the defendant" (i.e. to Phormio).

Quote II. Apollodorus vs Timotheus, Vol. V No. XLIX. Apollodorus speaking. Pasio's bank had slaves to receive and weigh articles given as security. [52]

The bank paid the freight on a shipment of lumber arriving for Timotheus. [29, 30]

Quote III. Callipus vs Apollodorus, Vol. V No. LII. Apollodorus speaking. When Lycon was about to sail to Libya he deposited 16 minas 4 drachmas in Pasio's bank. Phormio received and recorded the deposit. [5, 6] Lycon directed that the money was to be paid to his partner, Cephisiades, when Cephisiades arrived at Athens. [18, 24, 19] Callipus claims the money should have been paid to him. He is suing Apollodorus and his brother for the money. [30, 31] "It is the custom of all bankers, when a private person deposits money and directs that it be paid to a given person, to write down first the name of the person making the deposit and the amount deposited, and then to write on the margin 'To be paid to so and so;' and if he knows the face of the person to whom payment is to be made he merely does this, he writes down whom he is to pay; but, if he does not know it, it is the custom to write on the margin the name also of him who is to introduce and point out the person who is to receive the money." [4] Archebiades was to identify Cephisiades. [6, 7]

Quote IV. Apollodorus vs Polycles, Vol. VI No. L. Apollodorus speaking.
Apollodorus had continued acting as a trierarch beyond his appointed time, because Polycles, appointed as his successor, had not taken over. Apollodorus in so doing had incurred various expenses for which in this suit he was seeking reimbursement.
Concerning these expenses he said that he "had written down not only the disbursements themselves but also the objects for which the money had been spent, the nature of the service rendered, what the price was, in the coinage of what country the payment had been made, and what the loss in exchange was." For Professor Murray's translation of Apollodorus's last six words in this statement, ὁπόσου ἡ καταλλογὴ ᾖ τῷ αργυργίῳ I propose the following

alternative translation: "the cost of the foreign exchange." [30]

Quote V. Dareius vs Dionysodorus, Vol. VI No. LVI. Dareius speaking.

Dareius and Pamphilus made a loan of 30 minas to Dionysodorus and Parmeniscus for a voyage to Egypt and a return voyage to Athens. The ship was security. The return cargo was to be brought to Athens. Instead it was sold at Rhodes, and the ship, instead of returning to Athens, had been going back and forth between Rhodes and Egypt. Dareius is suing Dionysodorus for damages. There is some question whether Demosthenes wrote this oration. [Introduction]

Quote VI. Zenothemis vs Demo, Vol. IV No. XXXII. Demo speaking.

Note: Demo was the uncle of Demosthenes Jr., the orator, Protus had borrowed money from Demo in Athens which he used to finance the purchase in Syracuse of grain he planned to import into Athens. [18, 20, 21]

Protus and Zenothemis travelled from Athens to Syracuse on a ship captained by Hegestratus.

When the grain purchased by Protus was loaded on the ship Zenothemis and Hegestratus claimed it was owned by Zenothemis and borrowed money on it as security. They immediately sent [ἀπέστελλν] the money to Massalia (Marseilles) which was their home town. [4, 5]

They planned to sink the ship. Under the law at that time if the ship sank, they would be relieved of their debt obligations. Hegestratus was caught in the act of trying to cut a hole in the bottom of the ship. [5, 6]

He died trying to escape.

Note: ἀποστέλλω is used in connection with the sending of a message or the dispatching of a messenger.

Quote VII. Chrysippus and partner vs Phormio, Vol. IV No. XXXIV. Chrysippus speaking.

Note: The defendant is quite a different person from Phormio the banker.

Chrysippus and his partner had made a loan of 20 minas to Phormio to finance a voyage to Pontus and return.[6] The rate of interest was apparently 20%.

Phormio bought goods at Athens to sell at Pontus, apparently less than called for under the contract. He was having trouble selling what he had bought, and apparently sold it at a low price [7, 9] He did not load a return cargo at Pontus, though the contract called for doing so. He did not sail with Lampis, when Lampis started back from Pontus. [25] The ship was overloaded and was wrecked. The cargo and 30 lives were lost. Lampis escaped. [10] On reaching Athens Lampis stated that Phormio had not loaded a return cargo as the contract required and "had not paid the money to Lampis." [17] Later Lampis reversed his testimony re the return load and the repayment. [20] And Phormio now claimed that he had paid to Lampis at Bosphorus 120 Cyzicene staters. (This was equal to 33.6 minas at the exchange rate at that place. Cyzicus was on the shore of the Sea of Marmora.) [24] With no return cargo Phormio seems to have owed only 20.6 minas.

Phormio did not have as a witness to the payment either the partner of Chrysippus or his slave. He had letters to them that he had not delivered. His only witness was Lampis. [28, 29, 35] One Cyzicene stater was equal to 28 Athenian drachmas. [23]

Quote VIII. Androcles vs Lacritus, Vol. IV No. XXXV. Androcles speaking.

Artemo and Apollodorus of Phaselis in Asia Minor borrowed 30 silver minas from Androcles, an Athenian, and Nausicrates of a town in Euboea. The loan was made in Athens. Artemo and Apollodorus were to sail from Athens to Mende or Scione in the Chalcidice and there to buy and take on board ship 3,000 jars of wine and to sell it at Pontus and get a return cargo there to be sold at Athens. [10, 11, 18] The rate of interest was 25%, or if the voyage lasted after the middle of September it was 30%. Apollodorus took only 450 jars of wine aboard. [20] The proceeds of the sales at Pontus and Athens were to provide the money to pay the principal and interest on the loan. In violation of the loan agreement Artemo and Apollodorus borrowed 11 minas from Aratus in Halicarnassus. [22, 23] Apollodorus had no return cargo on board. [34] Apparently no money had been paid to Androcles and Nausicrates. Artemo had died and left his estate to his brother, Lacritus. The suit contended that Lacritus was liable for his brother's debts, also that (1) Artemo and Apollodorus had purchased less than 3,000 jars of wine, (2) they had failed to ship an adequate return cargo, (3) they had borrowed additional money using the wine as security, and (4) they had falsely asserted that the ship had been wrecked.

Exhibit C

The Works of Isocrates*

Quote I. The following statements were made by the plaintiff in a court in Athens. His name is not given; I shall refer to him as Anonym and the case as Anonym vs Pasio, Anonym speaking.

Professor Van Hook says in his introduction to this oration, which is entitled the Trapeziticus, or concerning the banker, that it "was written by Isocrates for a young man,

*Isocrates, *Orations and Letters,* vol. 3, trans. Larue Van Hook (Cambridge: Harvard University Press, 1945).

a subject of Satyrus, king of Bosporus (the Crimea of to-day), who accuses the banker Pasio of having appropriated a deposit of money which had been entrusted to him by the complainant."

I desired to travel abroad. And so my father loaded two ships with grain, gave me money, and sent me on a trading expedition and at the same time to see the world. Pythodorus, the Phoenician, introduced Pasio to me and I opened an account at his bank.   [4]
Satyrus arrested my father and sent orders to citizens of Pontus in residence here in Athens to take possession of my money and to bid me to return . . . . I related my troubles to Pasio . . . . . we decided that it would be best to agree to comply with all of Satyrus' demands and to surrender all the money whose existence was known, but with respect to the funds on deposit with Pasio we should not only deny their existence but also make it appear that I had borrowed money at interest both from Pasio and from others and to do everything which was likely to make them believe that I had no money . . . but . . . the sum of money on deposit with him was large.   [5, 7, 8]
When Stratocles was about to sail for Pontus, I, wishing to get as much of my money out of that country as possible, asked Stratocles to leave with me his own gold and on his arrival in Pontus to collect its equivalent from my father there, as I thought it would be highly advantageous not to jeopardize my money by the risks of a voyage, especially as the Lacedaemonians were then masters of the sea.   [35, 36]

A comment on this quotation suggests itself. Anonym thought this was a good way to get more money out of his father.

These things were done by me, not because of lack of funds, but that the parties in Pontus might believe that to be the case. . . . I will present to you first those who knew that I had received much money from Pontus; next, those who saw me as a patron of Pasio's bank; and besides, the persons from whom at that time I had bought more than a thousand gold staters. Pasio himself, moreover—in effect, at least—I will present as corroborating these statements. An information had been laid . . . against a trading-ship, upon which I had lent a large sum of money. . . . At first I was almost put to death without a trial; finally, however, they were persuaded to accept bondsmen from me. . . . Pasio . . . furnished for me Archestratus, the banker, as surety for seven talents. . . . It is obvious that Pasio . . . became my surety for seven talents because he judged that the gold on deposit with him was a sufficient guarantee.   [40, 41, 42, 43]

The staters Anonym bought were probably Cyzicene staters. One thousand would have been equal to about 280 Attic minas or 4 2/3 talents.

Notes

1. Chester G. Starr, *A History of the Ancient World* (New York: Oxford University Press, 1965), p. 372. Starr says trade declined after 350 B.C.

2. W. W. Tarn, *Hellenistic Civilization*, 3rd. ed. (New York: World Publishing, 1952), pp. 252–53; *Encyclopaedia Britannica,* 1929, vol. 6, p. 931; *Encyclopaedia Britannica,* 1968, vol. 17, p. 888; Starr, *Ancient World,* p. 368; George M. Calhoun, *The Business Life of Ancient Athens* (New York: Cooper Square Publishers, 1968), pp. 138–39.

3. Tarn, *Hellenistic Civilization,* p. 254. Tarn's *Hellenistic Civilization* is primarily concerned with the two hundred-odd years following the death of Alexander the Great. But the references in this and several of the following notes to pp. 253–61 are clearly pertinent to the whole of the fourth century.

4. Tarn, *Hellenistic Civilization,* pp. 253, 343; Catherine B. Avery, ed., *The New Classical Handbook* (New York: Appleton-Century-Crofts, 1962), p. 273; *Encyclopaedia Britannica,* 1929, vol. 2, p. 253; *Encyclopaedia Britannica,* 1968, vol. 2, p. 253.

5. Tarn, *Hellenistic Civilization*, pp. 254–55.

6. Tarn, *Hellenistic Civilization*, p. 255; Avery,*Classical Handbook*, p. 623.

7. Tarn, *Hellenistic Civilization*, p. 255.

8. Tarn, *Hellenistic Civilization*, p. 256; *Encyclopaedia Britannica*, 1929, vol. 9, p. 363; vol. 15, p. 198; vol. 20, p. 665; *Encyclopaedia Britannica*, 1968, vol. 9, p. 363; vol. 15, 198; vol. 20, p. 665.

9. Tarn, *Hellenistic Civilization*, p. 259; *Encyclopaedia Britannica*, 1929, vol. 17, pp. 246, 248.

10. Tarn, *Hellenistic Civilization*, p. 257; *Encyclopedia Britannica*, 1968, vol. 14, p. 859.

11. Tarn, *Hellenistic Civlization*, p. 258; *Encyclopaedia Britannica*, 1929, vol. 3, p. 168; vol. 6, p. 931; vol. 13, p. 852; *Encyclopaedia Britannica*, 1968, vol. 3, p. 168; vol. 6, pp. 931, 950; vol. 13, p. 852.

12. Tarn, *Hellenistic Civilization*, p. 258; *Encyclopaedia Britannica*, 1968, pp. 889, 893.

13. Tarn, *Hellenistic Civilization*, pp. 259, 261; *Encyclopaeida Britannica*, 1929, vol. 9, p. 688.

14. Calhoun, *The Business Life of Ancient Athens*, p. 45.

15. Tarn, *Hellenistic Civilization*, p. 255; *Encyclopaedia Britannica*, 1968, vol. 6, p. 143.

16. Starr, *Ancient World*, pp. 264–265, 388; *Encyclopaedia Britannica*, 1968, vol. 6, p. 143; Sir Lindsay Scott, "Pottery," in *A History of Technology*, eds. Charles Singer, E. J. Holmyard, and A. R. Hall (New York: Oxford University Press, 1954), vol. 1, pp. 408–409.

17. Tarn, *Hellenistic Civilization*, p. 251.

18. E. Victor Morgan, *A History of Money* (Baltimore: Penguin Books, 1965), p. 58.

19. Calhoun, *The Business Life of Ancient Athens*, pp. 138–139.

20. Morgan, *A History of Money*, p. 155. We shall use the word "polity" for both city-states and countries like Persia, Egypt and Macedonia.

21. Avery, *Classical Handbook*, p. 901.

22. Starr, *Ancient World*, p. 382.

23. Avery, *Classical Handbook*, p. 163; Calhoun, *The Business Life of Ancient Athens*, pp. 105, 125–126; *Encyclopaedia Britannica*, 1968, vol. 2, p. 391. Aristotle married Hermias' niece.

24. Morgan, *A History of Money*, p. 155.

25. Exhibit C, Quote I, Sections 35, 36; *Encyclopaedia Britannica*, 1929, vol. 10, p. 765; Tarn, *Hellenistic Civilization*, pp. 92, 174–176; Starr, *A History of the Ancient World*, pp. 312, 405; *Encyclopaedia Britannica*, 1968, vol. 17, p. 1100.

26. Exhibit B, Quote I, Sections 18, 20, 21.

27. Morgan, *A History of Money*, p. 155.

28. Exhibit B, Quote I; Quote II, Sections 29, 30; Quote III; Quote V; Exhibit C, Quote I, Sections 5, 7, 8, and 40, 41, 42, 43; Morgan, *A History of Money*, p. 58; Calhoun, *The Business Life of Ancient Athens*, especially pp. 91–94 and 100–105.

29. Exhibit B, Quote II, Section 52; Calhoun, *The Business Life of Ancient Athens*, pp. 91, 95.

30. Exhibit B, Quote V; Quote VI, Sections 4, 5, 18, 20, 21; Quote VII;

Quote VIII, especially Sections 10, 11, 118; Exhibit C, Quote I, Sections 4, 40, 41, 42, 43.

31. Exhibit B, Quote V; Quote VI, especially Sections 5, 6, 18, 20, 21; Quote VII; Quote VIII.

32. Exhibit B, Quote VI.

33. Exhibit B, Quote IV.

Chapter VI

Health Care in Ancient Times

We propose to inquire how medical science and health care practices developed in ancient times. We shall focus our attention on three geographical areas, Mesopotamia, Egypt, and Magna Graecia, and on the way developments in one of these areas affected developments in another. We shall be somewhat arbitrary about the time period we consider. We shall give no attention to anything that happened after 200 B.C.

There were significant developments in two other culture areas, China and the Indian subcontinent, during this period. In China during the Chou dynasty, probably from about 1122 to 250 B.C., a treatment for aches, pains, and other ailments called acupuncture was developed; this involved inserting a needle into an appropriate place in the patient's body and leaving it there for perhaps five or ten minutes. In the sixth century B.C., a doctor named Pien Ch'io introduced a method of diagnosing illnesses called sphygmology. This called for a minute observation of a patient's heartbeats. Pien Ch'io thought that a great many different types of beat could be distinguished, and that careful observation should enable the doctor to tell what was wrong with the patient.[1]

In India during the Brahman period, c. 800 B.C. to 700 A.D., there were skilled surgeons who performed difficult plastic surgery operations. The medical profession had a high

147

standard of professional ethics; a doctor was obligated to put the welfare of his patients above his own gain, to keep silent about the personal affairs of his patients, to have someone present when treating a woman patient. Toward the end of the sixth century B.C., as a result of the teachings of Buddha, a number of hospitals were established.[2]

In China, the knowledge of human anatomy was extremely limited. The dissection of a corpse was strictly forbidden. There seems to have been a prejudice against dissection in India, too. But there a surgeon would steep a corpse in water for a week to soften the tissues. The skin could then be brushed off to reveal the interior of the body. Thus, the Indian surgeons acquired a thorough knowledge of human anatomy.

Both in China during the Chou dynasty and in India during the Brahman period a technique for vaccinating a person against smallpox was developed; in each country the vaccine was made from matter taken from a sore on a person with a mild case. In China during the Chou dynasty, a man had to pass an examination in medicine before he could practice; in India he had to serve a long apprenticeship.[3]

We have singled out these medical developments in China and India as the developments most worth mentioning. Since there were no cultural contacts of consequence between China and the areas in which our interest centers and very slight contacts between India and these areas, we propose to dismiss China and India with having simply mentioned these selected developments.

Mesopotamia

The history of the medical profession begins in Sumer in the third millennium B.C. No doubt before that there had been, as there have been among various nonliterate peoples in historical times, witch doctors or medicine men who claimed to have some kind of divine assistance in curing illnesses.[4]

The Sumerians were the world's first literate people. Many

of them believed, as their ancestors had before them, that an illness was ordinarily a punishment inflicted by some god or demigod for an offense the ill person had committed. Accordingly, the steps taken to effect a cure included discovering the nature of the offense and taking actions to atone for it and to propitiate the deity who had been offended.

In ancient Sumer, the propitiation and atonement had quite early come to require the intervention of a priest or a baru (a diviner). The nature of the offense a person had committed might be divined by means of a sacrifice, often one in which the liver of the sacrificed victim was carefully studied. Atoning for the offense might call for appropriate offerings to the offended deity, and perhaps a ceremony to exorcise the demon of whom the ill person had become possessed.[5]

Priest-doctors continued to provide much the same type of ceremonial medical care in Mesopotamia for more than two thousand years. But this was by no means the only type of health care available. Perhaps as early as 2700 B.C., there were non-priest-doctors who were trained professional men, men trained in schools called *edubbas*. An edubba was, to begin with, a school for scribes that taught boys how to write and read the cuneiform script. In the course of time, it became a combination grammar school and institution of higher learning. For a young man who wanted to become a doctor, an *asu,* it offered instruction in what was then known about medicine, surgery, and pharmacology. No doubt only a fairly well-to-do father could afford for his son the kind of training an *edubba* provided.[6]

What we know about the medical practices of the Sumerians and also of the later Mesopotamians comes mostly from what is recorded on clay tablets in cuneiform script. For Sumer we do have, however, some roll seals with inscriptions that describe surgical instruments, and some bronze surgical knives and needles have survived.[7]

A particularly informative clay tablet dated c. 2200 B.C. was found at Nippur (now Nuffar) that records some fifteen recipes, eight for the preparation of poultices, three for medicines to be taken internally, and three for solutions with which a part of the body is to be washed. The fifteenth recipe is not very legible. The tablet throws a good deal of light on the medical materials used. Unfortunately, it does not tell us for what ailments the recipes were to be used. The author was evidently an *edubba*-trained doctor; no action by a divinity is suggested.[8]

There were several hundred plant and mineral items in the Sumerian pharmacopoeia, asafoetida, belladonna, colocynth, etc. By the time of the Third Dynasty of Ur (c. 2113 to 2006 B.C), the Sumerians had learned how to mix a fat and the ashes of a plant that contained a lot of soda to make a viscous soap. They used this as a salve.[9]

The clay tablets thus far deciphered tell us almost nothing about medical practice, but we can be reasonably certain that a Sumerian physician charged fees for his services, and that his income consisted of these fees. There was a physician who practiced at Lagash about 2000 B.C. and whose cylinder seal has been preserved. His name was Urlugaledinna. He held an important position under Ur-Ningirsu, who was at that time the ruler of the Lagash city-state. Professor Samuel N. Kramer thinks that at this time doctors "must have had a relatively high social status."[10]

There seems to be no satisfactory way to compare the importance of the service provided by priest-doctors with that of the services provided by *edubba*-trained physicians, or to compare the charges made for these two types of services. We may suspect, however, that the persons who were patients of physicians were, in general, in the upper income classes. We cannot say what proportion of the population had access to this kind of care. But we think it reasonable to suppose that in each of the Sumerian principal cities during the latter part of the third millennium B.C., there was at least one *edubba*-trained physician. Intercity rivalry doubtless made this the case.

We do not have much information about Sumerian surgery. During the Ur III period a bronze needle was used to remove cataracts. The Hammurabi Code of Law, written probably some time around the middle of the eighteenth century B.C., throws interesting light on operations performed in Babylon. Among other things, it prescribed the fees a surgeon should charge for various types of operations: ten shekels of silver for treating a severe wound with a knife and curing it if the patient was from the upper classes, two shekels if a slave. The Code also prescribed penalties to be imposed on a surgeon, if the patient died or suffered a severe injury. The Hammurabi Code was not the first code of law. It may have been copied in part from the code written by Ur-Nammu, who founded the Third Dynasty of Ur, or from one written by Lipit-Ishtar, who was king of Isin about 1930 B.C.[11]

One event—the writing of a letter—that occurred not many years before the writing of the Hammurabi Code is worth reporting, because it implies that people at that time understood the way a contagious disease could be communicated. The letter was from Kimri-Lim to his wife. He was king of Mari c. 1780 B.C., a great city situated on the Euphrates River more than two hundred miles above Sumer and Babylon. The translation of this letter reads in part: "Nanname has been taken ill . . . . Give severe orders that no one should drink in the cup where she drinks. . . . This disease is contagious."[12]

Medical progress was surely not helped by the continuing popular belief that an illness was commonly the act of a god or a demon. It may have been helped by the kind of training non-priest-doctors received; it is reasonable to suppose that the sound medical training of the Sumerian *edubba* was in some form maintained both in Babylonia and in Assyria. How much medical knowledge and practice had improved as a result by the time of Ashurbanipal, who ruled the Assyrian Empire c. 668 to 627 B.C., it would be difficult to say. We know that the pharmacopoeia had been considerably expanded. Assyrian doctors seem to have known a good deal about tuberculosis, pellagra, pneumonia, jaundice, intestinal obstructions, and strokes. Apparently they suspected a connection between mosquitoes and some kinds of fever. A great variety of surgical instruments and other medical items has been found at Nineveh. Some of the surgical instruments show that Assyrian surgeons did trepanations; we do not know why they did them. All in all the information we have indicates that from the time of Ur-Nammu to that of Ashurbanipal, there had been substantial progress in medical practice.[13]

Egypt

In Egypt, nearly everyone believed that an illness was ordinarily the act of a god or a demon. Priest-doctors treated people for illnesses; there were no non-priest-doctors. Medical care continued to be in the hands of priests until about the time of Alexander the Great.[14]

During the third dynasty, perhaps about 2700 B.C., King Zoser (or Djoser) commissioned one Imhotep to build what we know as the Stepped Pyramid. Imhotep was not only the king's vizier and an able architect-engineer; he was also a priest and a physician. After his death he was deified as the god of healing.[15]

Information about Egyptian medicine and diseases comes principally from papyri; but we have another source, too. Archeologists have learned from examining mummies that arthritis and decayed teeth were common ailments; and skeletons of persons suffering from osteomyelitis and spinal tuberculosis have been found. Examination of mummies has revealed also cases of arteriosclerosis and probably of appendicitis and gall and kidney stones. Chiefly through reports in papyri, we have learned about a good many other ailments from which Egyptians often suffered. Among them are: cholera, smallpox, and leprosy, also typhus, amoebic dysentery, malaria, and tuberculosis. And we should doubtless add the "Egyptian eye disease," trachoma.[16]

Egyptian priest-doctors were somewhat highly specialized. One man specialized in ailments of the belly, another in ailments of the eye, another in ailments of the teeth, and so on. This specialization may quite possibly have pushed in the direction of a careful observation and a systematic recording of

152

the circumstances under which ailments occurred. At all events, we have more than one papyrus roll that reports medical and surgical practices that thoroughly accord with a natural science approach.[17]

What has come to be identified as the Edwin Smith papyrus is of great interest. This is a copy, probably made in the seventeenth century B.C., of an older document; it is thought that the original was inscribed between 2700 and 2500 B.C. The copy is mainly concerned with surgery: the treatment of wounds with sutures and plasters, setting broken bones, strapping up a sprained arm or leg to hold it in place, cauterizing a wound. Ox bones were used as splints in setting a broken bone. The bandages were sometimes soaked in resin to make a kind of cast. In one case this scroll discusses, the patient had incurred a fracture that resulted in a paralysis of one side of his body. The surgeon confessed that he could not cure this ailment, but he planned to continue observing it. His comment on his patient is instructive; the translation reads: "Thou shouldst distinguish him from one whom something entering from outside has smitten." In other words, his patient was not to be regarded as one possessed by a demon but as one who had suffered a bodily injury the results of which ought to be observed dispassionately and in a matter-of-fact manner.[18]

Both the Edwin Smith papyrus and another known as the Ebers papyrus have comments on the importance of the heart for the life of the organism and on the way the heart was thought to "speak" in various parts of the body. A doctor made an observation on a patient called "measuring the heart." This was probably not exactly what we mean by taking a patient's pulse; but the doctor certainly must have noted whether the pulse was especially fast or slow.[19]

Beside the Edwin Smith papyrus, there were a number of other medical papyri that took a nonmagical, matter-of-fact approach. The Ebers papyrus was not one of these. In fact, the medical papyri in which magic and demons played a dominant role far outnumbered those that had something of a natural science viewpoint.[20]

The Egyptian pharmacopoeia was very extensive. Nearly

nine hundred prescriptions are said to have been recorded. It seems fair to say that Egyptian priest-doctors had learned how to provide a very superior kind of health care, a kind that was significantly better apparently than that provided by Mesopotamian doctors at that time. At all events, one very important person thought that that was the case c. 520 B.C. The Persians had made no significant contribution to the development of medical science; but their king was in a position to choose the best health care available. When Darius I ascended the throne, the court doctors who were brought to Susa to serve him were Egyptians, not Babylonians or Assyrians.[21]

We can assume that Egyptian physicians and surgeons were able to provide better medical care than those of Mesopotamia. But that does not mean that on the whole health care was better in Egypt than in Mesopotamia. We can be reasonably certain that the superior kind of health care Egyptian doctors could provide was available to only a small part of the population, probably only to important officials and their families and to other persons of high social status. We are particularly badly informed about the health care provided the fellahin, but it seems safe to assume that the priest-doctors did not give them a great deal of attention. We do not know what proportion of the population of Mesopotamia had access to the services of trained physicians and surgeons, but we think it must have been large enough to make the general level of health care better than was the case in Egypt.

In a sense, the history of ancient Egypt may be said to have ended about 306 B.C., when Ptolemy I became king. But we should probably add a note about the Hellenistic period in Egypt. Ptolemy I was a great patron of science and the arts. Among the men he attracted to the Museum he established in Alexandria were two Greek doctors, Herophilus of Calcedon and Erasistratus of Chios. Ptolemy made the bodies of recently executed criminals available to these two men for dissection. The result was that important scientific advances were made in both anatomy and physiology.[22]

But there is no reason to think that there was a significant improvement in health care for most people under Ptolemy I Soter (Savior), certainly not for the fellahin. And under his successors the lot of the fellahin worsened.[23]

Magna Graecia

The Iliad reports that Machaon and Podaleirios, sons of Aesclepius and both of them physicians like their father, were members of the expeditionary force against Troy. This was probably about 1200 B.C.[24]

The next physician we hear about was Democedes, a native of Croton who headed the medical school there toward the end of the sixth century B.C. Presently he moved, first to Aegina, then to Athens, and then to Samos. In all three places, he was a state employee.

Around 495 B.C. Persian forces captured Samos, and Democedes was taken as a slave to Susa. One day King Darius had an accident to his foot that was very painful. Herodotus tells us that "the ankle-bone was forced quite out of the socket." The Egyptian doctors who were his court physicians were unable to help him. According to Herodotus their treatment only made things worse. Darius learned about Democedes and required his services. Democedes, says Herodotus, "by using remedies customary among the Greeks . . . first enabled him to get some sleep, and then in a very little time restored him altogether." Thereafter, Democedes was royally treated; but he was still a prisoner. Not long after this, Atossa, the king's wife, had an abscess on her breast that he was able to cure. As a reward, he was sent on a spying expedition to Magna Graecia. He escaped, and so was enabled to satisfy his great desire. He had long wanted to return to Croton and live there. His success in dealing with the injury to the king's ankle reflected the fact that the knowledge and techniques of surgery in Greece at that time were substantially ahead of those of Egypt.[25]

Another native of Croton, Alcmaeon, was head of the Croton medical school during the early years of the fifth century. He studied physiology by dissecting organs and making ex-

155

periments. He discovered the optic nerve, and explored the nerve connections between the eye and other sense organs and the brain. He thought that the brain was the central organ of intelligence. His theory of disease was that it was the result of an organic disequilibrium. He wrote what was probably the first textbook on anatomy; unfortunately, only a few fragments have survived.[26]

Certainly by the time of Alcmaeon, Greek physicians had ceased to think of diseases as resulting from acts of gods and had come to assume that they could best be understood by making and recording observations of the physical circumstances under which the diseases occurred. The progress the Greeks made in medicine has been attributed to this natural science approach. However, it is only a partial explanation, for it does not account for the superiority of the Greeks as compared to their African and west Asian neighbors in surgery.[27]

Of course, there were still people in Greece who believed in cures that were acts of a god, particularly cures that were acts of Asclepius, who had become deified as the god of healing. We do not know just when this belief developed; but it was important in the fifth century, still more important in the fourth. There was a formal organization that propagated it, the Cult of Asclepius. In each community where there was a branch of this Cult, there was an area devoted to it called an Asclepion; a priest of Asclepius was in charge of it. The two principal buildings in the area were the temple dedicated to Asclepius and a kind of dormitory called the Abaton in which the healing ceremonies took place. There was a particularly prosperous and costly Asclepion at Epidaurus.[28]

A prospective patient who wanted to enter an Asclepion brought gifts, each according to his means. To be admitted he had to go through a purification ceremony; then he bathed and donned a white chiton. He was shown tablets on which were recorded cures performed by Asclepius. At night he slept in the Abaton, perhaps after the administration of a drug. While he slept he might be visited by Asclepius, perhaps accompanied by his daughter Hygeia. Sometimes while the patient slept a surgical operation was performed. In the morning he might or might not find that he was cured.[29]

During the fifth century B.C., there were a number of Asclepia; during the fourth, a number more. There were also men engaged in medical practice who considered themselves Asclepiads—lineal descendants of Asclepius—and who worshiped him as their patron god. There is disagreement among students of the history of medicine about the relation between Asclepiads and the priest-doctors who presided at the Asclepia.[30]

Partly because of this, what can be said with assurance about Hippocrates, who has been called the Father of Medicine, is very limited. He was born on the island of Cos c. 460 B.C. and spent the early years of his life there; he died in Larissa, Thessaly, sometime around 377 B.C. He was Hippocrates, Jr., the grandson of Hippocrates, Sr. His father, Heraclides, was a physician; he studied medicine under him as an apprentice. His nonmedical education included studying rhetoric under Gorgias, the sophist, and studying philosophy under Democritus. What is particularly interesting is that he went to Cnidus to study medicine under Herodicus. Thus he was exposed to ideas about medicine somewhat different from those of his father. The Cnidian school of medicine emphasized diagnosis, while the Coan school emphasized prognosis.[31]

Like many other physicians, Hippocrates considered himself to be an Asclepiad. Herbert S. Goldberg assumes that this meant that he served as a priest-doctor in an Asclepion at the temple at Cos.[32] Henry E. Sigerist, who presumably had the available archeological findings in mind when he wrote about it, says there was not even an altar to Asclepius at Cos until about 350 B.C., and no temple until about 300 B.C. And both he and Gerhard Venzmer insist that Asclepiads such as Hippocrates were not priests but physicians who relied on their medical prescriptions and their surgery plus the ability the human organism has for curing itself and made no pretense of having any supernatural therapeutic influence.[33]

What we know about medicine and medical practice in fifth-century Greece comes principally from what is called the

Hippocratic Collection. This consisted of some sixty odd books, documents, etc., all written in Ionic Greek. Many of the items in the Collection may have been originally properties of the medical school at Cos. Probably in the third century B.C., the Collection was assembled in the Library at Alexandria. What we have today has been pieced together from five manuscripts that had been held in Italian libraries in the tenth and eleventh centuries A.D. The texts of some twenty odd books and other items, together with English translations and extensive notes, have been published as a four-volume set by the Harvard University Press. The Collection includes items written by various authors; some of them may have been written before 450 B.C., some of them may have been written after 450 B.C., some of them two or three hundred years later than that. None of the items can be identified as certainly the work of Hippocrates.[34]

By far the most widely cited item in the Collection is what has come to be known as the Hippocratic Oath. We are not particularly concerned with this Oath, but we may note that, while some of its provisions set a high standard of professional ethics for doctors, the connection between it and Hippocrates is anything but close. Indeed, it is so remote that Dr. Sigerist concluded that this Oath is essentially non-Hippocratic. We agree with Dr. Sigerist.[35]

We are concerned to know what the differences among medical schools meant for health care, in particular how the medical and surgical practices of the Coan school differed from those of the Cnidian school. The emphasis the Cnidians put on diagnosis led them to identify a good many different diseases. One of the books in the Collection that was presumably written by a Cnidian doctor describes twelve diseases of the bladder and four of the kidneys. Medical thinking at that time had come to assume that there were different diseases that might need different medical treatment; but doctors had no definitive way of identifying the different diseases. The Cnidians may have identified too many diseases, the Coans too few. Indeed, the Coans seem to have acted as if there were only one acute disease, that is, one disease that gave patients high fevers.[36]

The book *Regimen in Acute Diseases,* which we assume was written by a Coan doctor, gives us an idea of the way such cases were handled. To begin with, the patient was given a purgative; except for laxatives, drugs were used sparingly. The patient was immediately put to bed and, except for going to the toilet, was kept there. He or she was put on a strict diet, usually just a barley gruel. The room was well aired but not drafty; it might be darkened. The bedding was sufficient to keep the patient warm. Cleanliness was thought important. Medicines were administered occasionally, often a mixture of honey and water or honey and vinegar. Hippocrates seems to have held that every acute disease had a common pattern which made prognosis—forecasting its course—possible. He put great emphasis on the capacity of the human body, given time, to cure itself. If and when a patient's fever subsided, he or she might be given other food and presently be permitted to get up. The Greeks had an extensive pharmacopoeia, much of it borrowed from Egypt and Mesopotamia, but since they did not have quinine or antibiotics, the way Coan physicians treated a disease they identified as acute was quite possibly equally appropriate for malaria, pneumonia, and amoebic dysentery. The treatment a Cnidian physician would have prescribed in the case of an acute disease was perhaps not so very different.[37]

A number of items in the Collection are concerned to describe the various types of surgical operations the Greeks performed and the surgical techniques they had developed. We shall not attempt to comment on them except to say that these items make it clear that Greek surgery was one of the major achievements of Greek civilization.[38]

We are not told about the fees a doctor charged, but doctors undoubtedly charged them. We may suspect that a successful doctor like Hippocrates had a pretty good income. Certainly he was well thought of and had a high social standing. Plato regarded Hippocrates as the intellectual equal of Phidias, the sculptor. In 429 B.C., he was called to Athens to help in fighting the plague from which the city was suffering.[39]

By the fourth century B.C., the Greeks had developed a very superior type of health care. We can only guess how many people were in a position to benefit by it, probably a larger proportion in Athens than in much of the rest of Magna Graecia. Venzmer gives the impression that in Athens at least it was available to most educated people, and that the kind of care asclepia provided was available to a good many others. Even if this was not entirely true, there must have been a very large number of people who were quite well cared for in Magna Graecia, a considerably larger fraction of the total population than had ever been the case before. But, in Greece and the rest of the Hellenistic world in the third century B.C., there were doubtless a great many people who were not so well provided for. Probably the most significant improvement in health care made during the last three centuries of the pre-Christian era was making the kind of health care the Greeks had developed available to a gradually increased percentage of the western world.

Notes

1. *Encyclopaedia Britannica,* 1929, vol. 5, p. 531; *Encyclopaedia Britannica,* 1968, vol. 1, p. 117; vol. 15, p. 94B; Gerhard Venzmer, *5000 Years of Medicine,* trans. Marion Koenig (New York: Taplinger Publishing Co., 1972; originally published Bremen: Carl Shunemann Verlag, 1968), pp. 44–47.

2. Venzmer, *5000 Years of Medicine,* pp. 55–57; *Encyclopaedia Britannica,* 1968, vol. 15, pp. 94, 94A.

3. Venzmer, *5000 Years of Medicine,* pp. 43, 44, 48, 53, 54, 56–57; *Encyclopaedia Britannica,* 1968, vol. 15, pp. 94, 94A.

4. Venzmer begins his book, *50000 Years of Medicine,* with a discussion of a painting of a medicine man on the wall of the cave of Les Trois Freres in the Pyrennes. According to Venzmer's reckoning, this medicine man "lived and worked more than seventeen thousand years ago." (See p. 16.)

5. Venzmer, *5000 Years of Medicine,* pp. 24–27; *Encyclopaedia Britannica,* 1929, vol. 2, p. 860; Georges Roux, *Ancient Iran* (Harmondsworth, Middlesex, England: Penguin Books, 1966; first published by George Allen and Unwin, 1964), p. 333.

6. Samuel H. Kramer, *The Sumerians: Their History, Culture and Character* (Chicago: University of Chicago Press, 1963), pp. 98–99, 230–31, 233; Roux, *Ancient Iraq,* p. 334; *Encyclopaedia Britannica,* 1929, vol. 2, p. 860; C.

Leonard Woolley, *The Sumerians* (London: Oxford University Press, 1929; reprint ed., New York: W. W. Norton & Co., 1965), pp. 108–11.

7. Kramer, *Sumerians*, p. 93; Venzmer, *5000 Years of Medicine*, pp. 22–23, 29.

8. Kramer, *Sumerians,* pp. 93–99, tenth plate following p. 64; Venzmer, *5000 Years of Medicine,* p. 22.

9. Martin Levey, *Chemistry and Chemical Technology in Ancient Mesopotomia* (London, New York, Princeton: Elsevier Publishing Company, 1959), p. 125; Venzmer, *5000 Years of Medicine,* pp. 22–23, 28–29; Kramer, *Sumerians,* pp. 95–97; Roux, *Ancient Iraq,* p. 336.

10. Kramer, *Sumerians,* p. 99.

11. Venzmer, *5000 Years of Medicine,* p. 27; Woolley, *The Sumerians,* p. 106.

12. Roux, *Ancient Iraq,* p. 337. He gives *sabtu* as the English script for the word he translates as "contagious" or "catching." Presumably it could not mean "accursed."

13. We are not informed about the medical books and documents in the great library Ashurbanipal assembled. This collection may well have been a significant help to doctors. See Roux, *Ancient Iraq,* pp. 298, 323–25. On the surgical instruments found at Nineveh, see Venzmer, *5000 Years of Medicine,* p. 29.

14. John A. Wilson, *The Culture of Ancient Egypt* (Chicago: University of Chicago Press, 1951), p. 58; Venzmer, *5000 Years of Medicine,* pp. 35–37.

15. *Encyclopaedia Britannica,* 1929, vol. 12, pp. 108–09; *Encyclopaedia Britannica,* 1968, vol. 8, p. 31; vol. 11, p. 1104; Venzmer, *5000 Years of Medicine,* pp. 33–34; Wilson, *Ancient Egypt,* p. 51.

16. Venzmer, *5000 Years of Medicine,* pp. 34–35; *Encyclopaedia Britannica,* 1968, vol. 8, p. 50.

17. Venzmer, *5000 Years of Medicine,* p. 36. See also Wilson, *Ancient Egypt,* pp. 55–58.

18. Wilson, *Ancient Egypt,* pp. 55–58; Venzmer, *5000 Years of Medicine,* pp. 38–39.

19. Wilson, *Ancient Egypt,* pp. 56–57.

20. Venzmer, *5000 Years of Medicine,* pp. 37–40.

21. Herodotus, *The History,* trans. George Rawlinson (New York: E. P. Dutton & Co., 1910), book III, chap. 129.

22. Venzmer, *5000 Years of Medicine,* pp. 87–90; Catherine B. Avery, ed., *The New Century Classical Handbook* (New York: Appleton-Century-Crofts, 1962), pp. 446, 560, 962; *Encyclopaedia Britannica,* 1929, vol. 8, p. 676; vol. 11, p. 516; vol. 15, p. 199.

23. W. W. Tarn, *Hellenistic Civilization,* 3rd. ed., rev. (New York: World Publishing, 1952), pp. 198–200.

24. Henry E. Sigerist, *A History of Medicine* (Oxford: Oxford University Press, 1962), vol. 2, pp. 26–32; Venzmer, *5000 Years of Medicine,* pp. 67–68; *Encyclopaedia Britannica,* 1968, vol. 15, p. 94B.

25. Herodotus, *The History,* book III, chaps. 129–38; Avery, *Classical Handbook,* pp. 385–86; Sigerist, *A History of Medicine,* pp. 84–89, 99–101.

26. Sigerist, *A History of Medicine,* pp. 101–4; Avery, *Classical Handbook,* p. 69; Venzmer, *5000 Years of Medicine,* pp. 69–70; *Enclyclopaedia Britannica,*

1929, vol. 3, p. 610; *Encyclopaedia Britannica*, 1968, vol. 1, p. 539.

27. Sigerist, *A History of Medicine*, pp. 84–89; Venzmer, *5000 Years of Medicine*, pp. 69–70.

28. *Encyclopaedia Britannica*, 1929, vol. 8, p. 649; *Encyclopaedia Britannica*, 1968, vol. 15, p. 94B; Avery, *Classical Handbook*, pp. 444, 829, 1105; Sigerist, *A History of Medicine*, pp. 62–63; Venzmer, *5000 Years of Medicine*, p. 71.

29. Sigerist, *A History of Medicine*, pp. 63–69; Venzmer, *5000 Years of Medicine*, p. 72; *Encyclopaedia Britannica*, 1968, vol. 15, p. 94B.

30. Sigerist, *A History of Medicine*, pp. 300–4; Venzmer, *5000 Years of Medicine*, pp. 76, 77.

31. Sigerist, *A History of Medicine*, pp. 268–71, 290; Venzmer, *5000 Years of Medicine*, pp. 73–74; Herbert S. Goldberg, *Hippocrates, Father of Medicine* (New York: Franklin Watts, Inc., 1963), pp. 17–18, 29, 79; Avery, *Classical Handbook*, p. 567; *Encyclopaedia Britannica*, 1929, vol. 11, p. 584; Hippocrates *(Collection)*, vol. 1, trans. W. H. S. Jones (Cambridge: Harvard University Press, 1923), p. xliv.

32. Goldberg, *Hippocrates, Father of Medicine*, pp. 29, 53.

33. Sigerist, *A History of Medicine*, pp. 58–59; Venzmer, *5000 Years of Medicine*, pp. 72, 76–77.

34. Hippocrates *(Collection)*, vol. 1, pp. xxviii ff., lxiii ff.; Sigerist, *A History of Medicine*, 264–67, 274–75; Venzmer, *5000 Years of Medicine*, pp. 76–77.

35. When we try to say what the connection was between Hippocrates and the Oath, we face serious difficulties. Of one thing we can be sure. Hippocrates did not require young men seeking admission to his school to take it. This Oath was apprently not written until after his death. The major problem about it, however, relates to what the taker pledges not to do. He pledges: (1) not to administer a poison to anyone when asked to do so; (2) not to give a woman a pessary to cause abortion; and (3) not to use a knife, even to remove a stone. None of these pledges accords with what was considered right and proper in fifth and fourth century Greece. Suicide was considered the honorable course for a man who thought he had no moral alternative. Abortions were common; infanticide was a general practice. And certainly it was morally proper for a doctor to perform a surgical operation. Sigerist, *A History of Medicine*, pp. 231, 302–4; Venzmer, *5000 Years of Medicine*, pp. 75–76; Goldberg, *Hippocrates, Father of Medicine*, pp. 93–95.

36. Sigerist, *A History of Medicine*, pp. 290–91; Venzmer, *5000 Years of Medicine*, p. 69.

37. Hippocrates *(Collection)*, vol. 2, trans. W. H. S. Jones (Cambridge: Harvard University Press) pp. 100 ff.; Sigerist, *A History of Medicine*, pp. 282–84.

38. Hippocrates *(Collection)*, vol. 3, trans. by E. T. Withington (Cambridge: Harvard University Press, 1928), pp. 100 ff.

39. Venzmer, *5000 Years of Medicine*, p. 74.

Chapter VII

Bank Demand Deposit Currency
Before 1700 A.D.

Bank deposits in checking accounts in commercial banks are the principal form of money in circulation in the United States today and the principal means used to pay commercial debts. This is true also in a number of other countries, British Commonwealth countries except India and Pakistan, and the industrialized countries of western Europe except possibly western Germany.[1]

Deposit money has been the principal form of money in circulation and means of paying commercial debts in these industrialized countries for only about a hundred years. Deposit money provides us a particularly convenient way of doing business and one that seems obvious now that we have it. One may wonder why it had not developed long before the late nineteenth century. Its recent development is easier to understand when we stop to think just what it involves.

Consider the payment of a debt by a check when A, the payee, deposits it in his bank and B, the drawer, drew the check on his checking account in some other bank. At the present time, the check is cleared through the Federal Reserve System. Not long after its establishment, in July 1916, the Federal Reserve banks took over the function of clearing checks. Let us take up first the situation in which the bank of

A, the payee, and B, the drawer, are in the same Federal Reserve district. In this event, we can think of the clearance as consisting of three steps: (1) the bank of A the payee that has credited the check to his checking account now deposits it in the Federal Reserve bank of the district; (2) the Federal Reserve bank next deposits it in the bank of B, the drawer; (3) this bank then charges the amount of the check to B's checking account and, probably with the end-of-the-month statement of his account, returns the now cancelled check to him for his record.

If the drawer's bank and the payee's bank are not in the same Federal Reserve district, the clearance of the check involves four steps instead of three: (1) the payee's bank deposits the check in the Federal Reserve bank of the district in which it is located; (2) this Federal Reserve bank deposits the check in the Federal Reserve bank of the district in which the drawer's bank is located; (3) the Federal Reserve bank of this district deposits it in the drawer's bank; (4) the drawer's bank charges it to the drawer's checking account. Beginning with 1919, the Federal Reserve System has published current reports on commercial debt payment made by check. These reports now give us each month fairly inclusive totals of such debt payments plus checks cashed and other amounts charged to demand accounts. The amounts so charged are called debits to individual accounts.[2]

At the present time, in general, the payee receives the full face amount of the check under this clearance arrangement. But this has not always been the case. Before July 1916, many banks had been charging a small fee for cashing a check on an out-of-town bank, and for some time thereafter a good many state banks continued to do so. Early in 1919, the Federal Reserve System adopted a program of establishing an arrangement under which all checks would be settled at par. There was opposition to this program; but by mid-1920, 94% of all commercial banks were settling at par.[3]

Before the Federal Reserve System clearing arrangements were established, there was a clearing house association in each major city. In any of these cities, when a man drew a check on his checking account in one bank to pay a debt to someone who had a checking account in another bank in the same city, the local clearing house association provided the clearance of the check; the check was simply debited to the account of the drawer's bank on the books of the clearing house and credited to the account of the payee's bank. The total amounts of checks handled in this way were called bank clearings. Although bank clearings did not include a commercial debt paid by check, when both the drawer and the payee had accounts at the same bank, the volume of debt payments recorded in bank clearings was very large. Before July 1916, bank clearings were taken as an indicator of the volume of commercial debts paid by check.[4]

When the payee's bank and the drawer's bank were located in two different cities, the payee's bank needed to have a correspondent relationship with a bank in the city in which the drawer's bank was located in order to arrange the clearance of the check. Let us call this correspondent Bank C. We can think of the clearance as involving first a deposit of the check by the payee's bank in Bank C, and then Bank C's putting the check through the clearing house where Bank C and the drawer's bank were located.

Since the payee's bank had already given the payee a credit to his bank account for the check, the face amount or that amount less the fee the bank charged, the process of its clearance in this case was essentially a series of reimbursements. We can think of the payee's bank as reimbursed by Bank C; Bank C as reimbursed by the clearing house; the clearing house as reimbrused by the drawer's bank; and the drawer's bank as reimbursed by the drawer. Of course, there was a contingency that this clearance arrangement had to provide for. The check was not presented to the drawer for settlement until some time after the payee had received payment, perhaps several days. The payment was in fact contingent on the completion of the clearance. It might be that the drawer's bank account was insufficient to cover the check and that the drawer had become bankrupt. In this event, the whole series of reimbursements was nullified and the payee had to return the payment he had received.[5]

When we realize how complicated the arrangements were that were needed for clearing a check in, say, 1890, it is easy to understand why it was so long before they developed. There were, however, arrangements something like them in times past. We propose to inquire about these arrangements; we shall call them earlier forms of bank deposit money. We shall try to say not only when and where they developed, but also what they were like.

About 300 or 200 B.C., in ancient Egypt, there was a kind of bank deposit money in use. Apparently it circulated quite widely. The central bank at that time was in Alexandria. It was a State Bank, a government enterprise closely affiliated with the royal treasury. It was a monopoly; it had branches in other places. There were deposit accounts in the central bank and its various branches that it seems proper to call demand accounts. We know that a depositor could draw on his or her account to pay a debt owed to a local merchant. We do not know what form the draft took.

A second-century papyrus record, Teb 891.36, contains fragments of the daily accounts kept by a small branch bank in the Heracleopolite nome. The payments the bank made on the order of its depositors are recorded. Rostovtzeff says of them, "In many instances . . . the payments were effected by transfer from one account to another without money passing. . . . I mention this detail . . . because many eminent scholars have thought it improbable that such transfers were made in ancient times." In this record the names of some persons are in the genitive case, of others in the dative; it has not been determined whether this distinguished debit entries from credits. In any event, it seems clear that when a debtor paid his debt his deposit account in the State Bank was debited and the creditor's account was credited and that no specie changed hands. A system of settling commercial debts a good deal like our present system was in operation.[6]

However, a significant point of difference should be noted. The State Bank of Egypt was quite possibly a complete monopoly. If it was, there was no need for any arrangement for interbank settlements. To be sure we cannot be certain that the monopoly was complete. But if there were one or more private banks, each of them must have had a deposit account in the central State Bank, and if so, this would have made provision for the simple kind of interbank settlement arrangement needed under the circumstances.

Except for this monopoly situation and except that the Egyptian arrangements in the second and third centuries B.C. for the payment of commercial debts were purely domestic business arrangements, they were quite closely similar to ours today. But the Egyptian banking system was in this respect something of an anomaly. There was nothing else that as closely resembled the way we now handle commercial debt payments for a good many years.

In much of the rest of the Hellenistic World, business activities were in other respects more like our modern business activities than were those of ancient Egypt. Certainly in rural Egypt, much economic activity was on a nonmoney basis, while there were many Greek city-states that were definitely money economies. Rhodes at this time was the commercial and banking center of the whole Mediterranean area. We know very little about Rhodesian banks. They must have been pretty much like the banks in Athens and other places about which we have quite a bit of information. We would probably be safe in assuming that more than one of them did a larger volume of international banking business than the State Bank in Alexandria did. Rhodesian bankers undoubtedly knew about the way the Egyptian banking system operated. If they did not adopt Egyptian practices in the making of commercial debt payments, the obvious explanation—though it is not a complete one—is that they could not do so because no Rhodesian bank had a monopoly. Under these circumstances an arrangement for paying commercial debts anything like ours would have involved the necessity for some kind of clearing house to handle interbank settlements. Since there was no such clearing house, an arrangement anything like ours was impossible.[7]

At least by the fourth century B.C., Greek banks were accepting deposits, probably non-interest-bearing deposits on current account. They also did a safety deposit business. And a banker occasionally provided surety for a customer in whom he had confidence. He made payments on a customer's order, and he acted as a collection agent. Perhaps his principal banking activity was making loans, particularly mortgage loans on local real estate. He was still a money-changer who converted the currency issued by one polity into currency issued by another. Probably a much more important function that he performed in the fourth century was providing a customer with money circulating in another polity in the form of a deposit in a bank in that polity. We assume he was able to do this by virtue of having a correspondent relationship with that bank. One thing he apparently did not do was to transfer on the order of a customer to another party a deposit that stood to the credit of that customer. Even in the second century B.C., Greeks banks did not provide this way of paying a commercial debt.[8]

Roman banks in the second century A.D. did. Roman bankers probably knew how the Egyptian banking system operated three or four hundred years earlier, and they may have taken a cue from it. The debt payment arrangement they developed involved no credit instruments. The debtor gave his bank an oral order to use his deposit account to pay his debt. But giving the order was not as simple as writing a check. He had to give the order before a notary, who made an official record of it. There must have been a good many such orders issued at this time, for there were notaries especially appointed for recording them. This method of paying commercial debts made a current deposit in a bank serve as a kind of bank deposit money. If the bankers had any arrangement for offsetting the debts one banker paid against those paid by other bankers, we are not informed about it. Bankers ceased to provide this type of bank deposit money probably sometime before the Roman Empire came to an end in 476 A.D.[9]

The parts of western Europe that emerged first from the Middle Ages were the port cities of the western Mediterranean. By 1200 A.D., there were banks in a number of them that accepted deposits on current account, among them Venice, Genoa, Florence, and Barcelona. All of the principal port cities on the western Mediterranean presently enacted ordinances that required that a bank, before it could do a current deposit business, must post a substantial bond to guarantee the ready convertibility of its deposits into specie.[10]

At least by 1300 each bank was keeping journals and ledger accounts that provided an up-to-date record of the balance of each depositor's account. We assume that debit and credit entries were posted currently to it. The bank made a payment to any party on a depositor's order and from time to time converted some of his deposit into cash. It probably often acted as a collection agent on his behalf. No kind of credit instrument was employed at this time in the dealings between a banker and his customer; the customer's orders were all given orally. The entry of an agreement between a banker and his client in the banker's journal was legal proof of the agreement. A binding contract could be made orally. A banker probably acted as surety for a customer in whom he had confidence, when the customer had occasion for this type of service. And bankers doubtless did a safety deposit business. At least in Barcelona, in the fifteenth century, most banking firms were partnerships with two or three partners. Some firms may have engaged in trade as well as in a banking business.[11]

A thirteenth or fourteenth century banker often held a formal power of attorney for a client. His deposits provided him with funds that he could lend. The collateral he held as security for a loan often took the form of jewelry, plate, and other kinds of saleable personalty. The cash reserves he maintained against his deposit liabilities we should consider very large, probably often more than 30%. Also, he probably charged what we should consider a high rate of interest, perhaps 25% or more.[12]

Much of the business of a bank during the thirteenth and

fourteenth centuries was transacted at a temporary stall or bench that had little in the way of shelter from bad weather. The stall was in a central business location; in Venice, the bankers had tables at the Rialto. The permanent locus of a bank was commonly the dwelling house of the senior member of the firm. The books of the bank and the moneybags were brought out to the stall or table in the morning and taken home at night.[13]

The principal early credit instruments were the bill of exchange and the check. The former was used extensively from the middle of the fourteenth century on. It was a holographic document for some time; that is to say, the whole document had to be in the handwriting of the maker and on paper bearing his personal seal or other identifying symbol. Early in the sixteenth century, bills of exchange began losing their holographic character; there were bills signed only by a clerk or associate of the principal. Checks do not seem to have been widely used until about 1500. Neither the bill of exchange nor the check was a negotiable instrument until the late sixteenth century or sometime in the seventeenth. Before that, the payee had to appear in person to receive the amount due him or to be represented by an authorized agent. Presumably, he might be paid either in specie or in the form of a credit to his bank account.[14]

A bank commonly had deposits to its credit in other banks, both banks in the city in which it was situated and banks in other places. This made it possible for a depositor to make a payment by check to a party who had an account at another bank, or who lived in another city. Quite possibly as early as the thirteenth century, a banker must have had correspondent relationships with bankers in various other places and was providing his customers with foreign exchange. When a banker sold a customer a deposit in a bank in another polity, he had to have a correspondent relationship with a banker in that polity, and this would seem to require that he should be able to write a check or a sight draft that drew on his account with that correspondent. I think, therefore, that this kind of credit instrument must have developed by the thirteenth century to make the interpolity trade at that time possible. Presumably, a banker who dealt in foreign exchange continued to do a little money-changer business. A man who wanted to travel to another polity would need both a draft on a bank in that polity and a little pocket money of the kind circulating there.[15]

In one Mediterranean city, Venice, there was a form of bank deposit money as early as the fourteenth century. There were apparently only four or five banking houses that had stalls at the Rialto at that time. Each of them did a current deposit business; accepting deposits on current account seems to have been the most important banking function. Depositors maintained such accounts mainly because this provided a particularly convenient way to make payments to and receive payments from other parties. When Depositor X in Bank A made a payment to Y, his account with Banker A was debited, and Y's account was credited. To effect this transfer of credit, X had to appear in person before Banker A and direct the transfer. Banker A then "wrote as directed in his book, which was an official notarial record." No written credit instrument like a modern check was involved. In Venice, everyone "of any consequence in business had an account so that he could make and receive payments through the banks. They were called *banche di scrita* or *del giro* because their main function was to write transfers and thus to rotate (*girare*) credits from one account to another." It is clear that these deposits on current account were a form of bank deposit money. Of course, they provided the banks with funds that they invested.[16]

This type of banking, giro-banking, probably continued without any very great change through most of the eighteenth century. We are informed principally about the bankers. We do not know how large the reserves were that they held toward the end of the fifteenth century, or how many of them there were. We assume their reserves were substantial. But one of the banks failed in 1499, and runs on the others followed. Apparently only one of them, the bank of Alvise Pisano, survived. During the early years of the sixteenth century he seems

171

to have had close to a monopoly. Presently there were doubtless competitors. Probably after his death in 1528, the Pisano-Tiepolo Bank continued for a time to be the most important one. But it failed dramatically in 1587, and a public bank, the Banco della Piazza di Rialto, was established. This institution was given a monopoly; apparently it provided much the same type of bank deposit money the private banks had been providing. However, it seems to have been in financial difficulties at a time when Venice was having trouble borrowing: "To meet the difficulties of the state . . . the Banco Giro was formed in Venice in 1619." We assume that thereafter, for a time, the Banco Giro provided Venetians with the kind of deposit money to which they had become accustomed. In 1638, the Banco della Piazza and the Banco Giro were combined; this combined institution continued to operate until 1806.[17]

It seems clear that deposit accounts in these public giro-banks as well as deposits in their private predecessors served as a form of bank deposit money. However, there is one point about them on which we should.like to be informed but are not. When there were four or five competing private banks in operation, there must have been a problem of making arrangements for interbank settlements, of effecting interbank clearings. And during any period when both public banks were in operation, there was a problem of arranging interbank clearings, too. The problem in the case of the two public banks was doubtless easily worked out. With four or five private bankers, it was more complicated. But they must have been well acquainted with each other; they may quite possibly have been friends. It is difficult to believe that, with only four or five of them, they did not have some kind of interbank clearing arrangement. Still, if we do not know how the Venetians handled the problem of interbank settlements in the fourteenth century and the early sixteenth, we can be quite sure that giro-banks provided them with a kind of bank deposit money for more than three centuries. This may well have been the principal kind of money in circulation in Venice in a period in which Venice was a major international financial center and in which bills of exchange drawn in many places in western Europe were presented in Venice for payment.

Notes

1. *The United Nations Statistical Yearbook* carries a money-supply table each year that shows for each of forty-odd countries currency (notes and coin) and deposit money (deposits with money-creating banks and other deposits subject to cheque), table 166. In each of these countries except West Germany, the total of deposit money is substantially larger than the total of currency. In West Germany, the two totals have been about the same, currency larger in some years, deposit money larger in others. In several of the less industrialized countries, the currency total has been considerably larger than the deposit money total.

2. Harold G. Moulton, *The Financial Organization of Society,* 2nd ed. (Chicago: University of Chicago Press, 1925), pp. 585–89; *Historical Statistics of the United States, Colonial Times to 1957* (Washington, D.C.: Government Printing Office, 1960), Series X 216. For some time now, the reports on debits to individual accounts have covered 233 of the 266 standard metropolitan statistical areas into which the country has been divided. The population of these 233 areas in 1970 was 98.5% of the U.S. total. We can safely assume that currently the total of debits to individual accounts in these areas is at least 98.5% of the U.S. total.

3. Moulton, *Financial Organization,* pp. 589–91.

4. For New York City, annual figures on bank clearings are available beginning with the year ending September 30, 1854. For all cities reporting to the New York Clearing House Association, annual figures are available for years beginning with the year October 1, 1881 to September 30, 1882. See *Historical Statistics,* Series X 227, X 228, and X 229.

5. Moulton, *Financial Organization,* p. 452.

6. M. Rostovtzeff, *Social and Economic History of the Hellenistic World* (Oxford: Oxford University Press, 1941), especially pp. 404–6, 1276, and 1285. See also E. Victor Morgan, *A History of Money* (Baltimore: Penguin Books, 1965), p. 22; W. W. Tarn, *Hellenistic Civilization* (New York: World Publishing, 1952), p. 192. The provinces into which ancient Egypt was divided were called nomes.

7. Tarn, *Hellenistic Civilization,* p. 175; Rostovtzeff, *Hellenistic World,* p. 680.

8. George M. Calhoun, *The Business Life of Ancient Athens* (New York: Cooper Square Publishers, 1968), chap. IV. See also Morgan, *A History of Money,* p. 22; *Encyclopaedia Britannica,* 1968, vol. 3, p. 93.

9. A. P. Usher, *The Early History of Deposit Banking in Mediterranean Europe* (New York: Russell and Russell, 1943), pp. 4, 5; Morgan, *A History of Money,* p. 22; *Encyclopaedia Britannica,* 1968, vol. 3, p. 93.

10. Usher, *Deposit Banking,* pp. 3, 17; Morgan, *A History of Money,* p. 22; *Encyclopaedia Britannica,* 1968, vol. 3, p. 93.

11. Usher, *Deposit Banking,* pp. 13–14, 18, 19, 237–40, 250–54; Frederic

173

C. Lane, *Venice: A Maritime Republic* (Baltimore: Johns Hopkins University Press, 1973), pp. 140–41. The double-entry system of bookkeeping was developed during the fourteenth century, perhaps in Genoa and Florence. The journals and ledger accounts a bank kept provided an up-to-date record of each depositor's account that had legal validity. The development of financial statements of the condition and operations of a bank or other business did not come until later. There were evidently serious questions about the adequacy and even the accuracy of sixteenth-century bank records. Usher thinks a banker must have made many mistakes "due to the ignorance of the condition of the bank." There were few bank balance sheets before 1600.

12. Usher, *Deposit Banking,* pp. 14, 181, 338.

13. Usher, *Deposit Banking,* pp. 12–13; Lane, *Venice: A Maritime Republic,* p. 147.

14. Usher, *Deposit Banking,* pp. 6–7, 9, 73–78, 89–90; Lane, *Venice: A Maritime Republic,* p. 141.

15. Usher, *Deposit Banking,* pp. 20, 183–87, 249–50.

16. Lane, *Venice: A Maritime Republic,* p. 147.

17. Lane, *Venice: A Maritime Republic,* pp. 327–30; *Encyclopaedia Britannica,* 1968, vol. 3, p. 93.

Bibliography

Allchin, Bridget and Raymond. *The Birth of Indian Civilization.* Baltimore: Penguin Books, 1968.

Avery, Catherine B., ed. *The New Century Classical Handbook.* New York: Appleton-Century-Crofts, 1962.

Braidwood, Robert J. Article on prehistoric villages on the Kurdistan Steppe, Iran. In *Encyclopaedia Britannica,* 1968, vol. 2, pp. 234–35.

Brinkman, J. A. Appendix to *Ancient Mesopotamia: Portrait of a Dead Civilization,* by A. Leo Oppenheim. Chicago: University of Chicago Press, 1964. Mesopotamian chronology of the historical period.

Bromehead, C. N. "Mining and Quarrying." In *A History of Technology,* edited by Charles Singer, E. J. Holmyard, and A. R. Hall, vol. 1, p. 591. New York: Oxford University Press, 1954.

Buxton, L. H. Dudley. "Mesopotamia." In *Encyclopaedia Britannica,* 1929, vol. 15, p. 288.

Calhoun, George M. *The Business Life of Ancient Athens,* New York: Cooper Square Publishers, 1968.

Childe, V. Gordon. "Rotary Motion." In *A History of Technology,* edited by Charles Singer, E. J. Holmyard, and A. R. Hall, vol. I, V, p. 105. New York: Oxford University Press, 1954.

———. *Social Evolution.* New York: Schuman, 1951.

———. "Wheeled Vehicles." In *A History of Technology,* edited by Charles Singer, E. J. Holmyard, and A. R. Hall. New York: Oxford University Press, 1954, p. 721.

Cole, S. M. "Land Transport Without Wheels." In *A History of Technology,* edited by Charles Singer, E. J. Holmyard, and A. R. Hall, vol. 1, p. 714. New York: Oxford University Press, 1954.

———. "Roads." In *A History of Technology,* edited by Charles Singer, E. J. Holmyard, and A. R. Hall, vol. 1, p. 713. New York: Oxford University Press, 1954.

Crowfoot, Grace M. "Textiles, Basketry, and Mats." In *A History of Technology,* edited by Charles Singer, E. J. Holmyard, and A. R. Hall, vol. 1, p. 418. New York: Oxford University Press, 1954.

de Gobineau, J. A. *The World of the Persians*. Geneva: Editions Minerva, 1971.

Demosthenes. *Private Orations*. Translated by A. T. Murray. Cambridge: Harvard University Press, vol. 4, 1936, vol. 5 and 6, 1939.

Digby, Adrian. "Boats and Ships." In *A History of Technology*, edited by Charles Singer, E. J. Holmyard, and A. R. Hall, vol. 1, p. 733. New York: Oxford University Press, 1954.

Drower, M. J. "Water-supply, Irrigation, and Agriculture." In *A History of Technology*, edited by Charles Singer, E. J. Holmyard, and A. R. Hall, vol. 1, pp. 531–34. New York: Oxford University Press, 1954.

Forbes, R. J. "Chemical, Culinary, and Cosmetic Arts." In *A History of Technology*, edited by Charles Singer, E. J. Holmyard, and A. R. Hall, vol. 1, pp. 247–48. New York: Oxford University Press, 1954.

Fuller, Major General J. F. C. *The Generalship of Alexander the Great*. New York: Funk & Wagnals, 1968 paperback; published by arrangement with Rutgers University Press, © 1960.

Goldberg, Herbert S. *Hippocrates, Father of Medicine*. New York: Franklin Watts, 1963.

Gordon, Cyrus H. *The Ancient Near East*. Rev. ed. New York: W. W. Norton & Co., 1965.

Grimal, Pierre. *Hellenism and the Rise of Rome*. New York: Delacorte Press, 1965.

Gurney, O. R. *The Hittites*. Baltimore: Penguin Books, 1952.

Güterbock, Hans G. "Babylonia and Assyria: History." In *Encyclopaedia Britannica,* 1968, vol. 2, p. 968.

Hayes, William C. *Most Ancient Egypt*. Chicago: University of Chicago Press, 1965.

Herodotus. *The History*. Translated by George Rawlinson. 2 vols. London: J. M. Dent and Sons; New York: E. P. Dutton & Co., 1910.

Herskovits, Melville J. *Economic Anthropology*. New York: W. W. Norton & Co., 1965 paperback; published by arrangement with Alfred A. Knopf, Inc.; originally published as *The Economic Life of Primitive Peoples,* 1940.

Hippocrates. *Collection*. Vol. 1 and 2 translated by W. H. S. Jones; Vol. 3 translated by E. T. Withington. Cambridge: Harvard University Press, vols. 1 and 2, 1923; vol. 3, 1928.

Historical Statistics of the United States, Colonial Times to 1957. Series X 216, X 227, X 228, X 229. Washington, D.C.: Government Printing Office, 1960.

Hole, Frank C. "Evidences of Social Organization from Western Iran." In *New Perspectives in Archeology*. Sally R. and Lewis R. Binford. Chicago: Aldine Publishing Co., 1968.

Hooke, S. H. "Recording and Writing." In *A History of Technology*, edited by Charles Singer, E. J. Holmyard, and A. R. Hall, vol. 1, p. 753. New York: Oxford University Press, 1954.

Hutchinson, R. W. *Prehistoric Crete*. Baltimore: Penguin Books, 1962.

Isocrates. *Orations and Letters*, vol. 3. Translated by Larue Van Hook. Cambridge: Harvard University Press, 1945.

Kramer, Samuel N. *The Sumerians: Their History, Culture and Character*. Chicago: University of Chicago Press, 1963.

Lane, Frederic C. *Venice: A Maritime Republic*. Baltimore: Johns Hopkins University Press, 1973.

Levey, Martin. *Chemistry and Chemical Technology in Ancient Mesopotamia*. New York, London, Princeton: Elsevier Publishing Co., 1959.

Mallowan, M. E. I. *Early Mesopotamia and Iran*. New York: McGraw-Hill Book Co., 1965.

Marx, Karl. *Capital*. Trans. from 3rd German ed. by S. Moore and E. Aveling. Chicago: Charles H. Kerr & Co., 1906.

Mason, J. Alden. *The Ancient Civilizations of Peru*. Hammondsworth, Middlesex, England: Penguin Books, 1957.

Mellaart, James. *Early Civilizations in the Near East*. New York: McGraw-Hill Book Co., 1965.

Morgan, E. Victor. *A History of Money*. Baltimore: Penguin Books, 1965.

Moulton, Harold G. *The Financial Organization of Society*. 2nd ed. Chicago: University of Chicago Press, 1925.

Neugebauer, O. "Ancient Mathematics and Astronomy." In *A History of Technology*, edited by Charles Singer, E. J. Holmyard, and A. R. Hall, vol. 1, p. 790. New York: Oxford University Press, 1954.

Oppenheim, A. Leo. *Ancient Mesopotamia: Portrait of a Dead Civilization*. Chicago: University of Chicago Press, 1964.

Perkins, Ann Louise. *The Comparative Archeology of Early Mesopotamia*. Chicago: University of Chicago Press, 1949.

Prescott, Willaim H. *The World of the Incas*. Geneva: Editions Minerva, 1970.

Rostovtzeff, M. *Social and Economic History of the Hellenistic World*. Oxford: Oxford University Press, 1941.

Roux, Georges. *Ancient Iraq*. Harmondsworth, Middlesex, England: Penguin Books, 1966; first published by George Allen & Unwin, 1964.

Scott, Sir Lindsay. "Pottery." In *A History of Technology*, edited by Charles Singer, E. J. Holmyard, and A. R. Hall, vol. 1, pp. 408–409. New York: Oxford University Press, 1954.

Sigerist, Henry E. *A History of Medicine*. Oxford: Oxford University Press, 1962.

Skinner, F. G. "Measures and Weights." In *A History of Technology*, edited by Charles Singer, E. J. Holmyard, and A. R. Hall, vol. 1 pp. 774–81. New York: Oxford University Press, 1964

Starr, Chester G. *A History of the Ancient World*. New York: Oxford University Press, 1965.

Steward, Julian H. *Theory of Cultural Change*. Normal, Ill.: University of Illinois Press, 1962.

Tarn, W. W. *Hellenistic Civilization*. 3rd ed., rev. New York: World Publishing, 1952.

Tcherikover, Victor. *Hellenistic Civilization and the Jews*. New York: Atheneum, 1959.

Thucydides. *History of the Peloponnesian War*. Translated by Richard Crawley. New York: E. P. Dutton & Co., 1910.

Usher, A. P. *The Early History of Deposit Banking in Mediterranean Europe*. New York: Russell and Russell, 1943.

Veblen, Thorstein. *Imperial Germany and the Industrial Revolution*. New York: Macmillan Co., 1915.

Venzmer, Gerhard. *5000 Years of Medicine*. Translated by Marion Koenig. New York: Taplinger Publishing Co., 1972; originally published Bremen: Carl Shunemann Verlag, 1968.

Von Hagen, Victor W. *Realm of the Incas*. Rev. ed. New York: New American Library, 1957.

Wilson, John A. *The Culture of Ancient Egypt*. Chicago: University of Chicago Press, 1951; first paperback ed., 1956.

Wolley, C. Leonard. *The Sumerians*. London: Oxford University Press, 1928; reprint ed., New York: W. W. Norton & Co., 1965.

Xenophon. *Anabasis*. Rev. ed. Edited and with an introduction by William W. Goodwin and John Williams White; Greek-English dictionary by John Williams White and Morris H. Morgan. Boston: Ginn & Co., 1894.

Yearbook of National Accounts Statistics, 1969, Volume I, Individual Country Data, United Nations, New York, 1970.

Index

Erasistratus, 154
Erech (Uruk, Warka), 10, 19, 73–4, 79
Eritrea, 116
Esarhaddon, 109
Eshnunna, 81–2
Euphrates, 106, 151

Federal Reserve system, 163ff.
fellahin, 30–1, 36, 61, 154–5
ferries, 53
Fertile Crescent, 12, 15, 19, 65, 75
frankincense, 131

Gadir (Cadiz), 100, 130
Gaza, 124
Gilgamish, 73
Giro, Banco, 171
giro banks, 171ff.
Granicus, 69
grappling iron, 98
Greeks, 116–7, 120
Gutians, 79, 80, 82

Halaf period, 10
Hammurabi, 82ff.
Hammurabi Code, 150–51
handicrafts 11–2, 16, 109
"hanging gardens," 113
hegemon, 120
Hegestratus, 133, 135, 140
Heracleopolite branch bank, 166
Hermias, 131, 133
Herodicus, 157
Herophilus, 154
hieroglyphs, 32
highways, Inca, 49ff
Hippocrates (elder), 157
Hippocrates (younger), 157–9
Hippocratic Collection, 158
Hippocratic Oath, 158
Hittites, 67, 86ff.
horse, 17, 86, 91
Hydaspes, 126–7
Hygeia, 156

Hyksos, 86–88

Iahdum-Lim, 82
Ibbi-Sin, 81
Illyria, 120
Imhotep, 32, 152
implements, 18
Incas, 41, 43, 46
Inca Empire, 41ff.
Inca, Pachacuti, 40
Inca, Topo, 41
Ionia, 116, 121, 130
India, doctors in, in the Brahmin period, 147
iron weapons, 104
irrigation systems, 11, 20, 61, 109, 113
    in Egypt, 31, 37
    Inca, 46, 51
Isin, 81, 151
Isocrates, 120, 142
Israel, 100
Issus, 69

Jerusalem, 106, 113
Judah, 100, 113

Kimri-Lim, 151
Kish, 74

Labarnes I, 88
Lagash, 73–4, 150
Laodicea, 130
Larissa, 157
Laurium, 130, 132
League of Corinth, 120, 123
Lipit-Ishtar, 81, 151
llamas, 42, 52–3
lugal, 74
Lugalanda, 75
Lugalzaggesi, 75, 77

Macedonians, 120ff, 130–31
Machaon, 155
Machu Picchu, 49

	DATE DUE		